PORTRAIT OF MURDER

A Drama

by

ROBERT BLOOMFIELD

SAMUEL  FRENCH

LONDON
NEW YORK TORONTO SYDNEY HOLLYWOOD

Copyright © unpublished under title *The Unremembered* DU 51519
15th August 1960 by Robert Bloomfield
Copyright © 1964 revised by Robert Bloomfield
All Rights Reserved

PORTRAIT OF MURDER is fully protected under the copyright laws of the British Commonwealth, including Canada, the United States of America, and all other countries of the Copyright Union. All rights, including professional and amateur stage productions, recitation, lecturing, public reading, motion picture, radio broadcasting, television and the rights of translation into foreign languages are strictly reserved.

ISBN 978-0-573-01351-5

www.samuelfrench.co.uk
www.samuelfrench.com

FOR AMATEUR PRODUCTION ENQUIRIES

UNITED KINGDOM AND WORLD
EXCLUDING NORTH AMERICA
plays@SamuelFrench-London.co.uk
020 7255 4302/01

Each title is subject to availability from Samuel French, depending upon country of performance.

CAUTION: Professional and amateur producers are hereby warned that PORTRAIT OF MURDER is subject to a licensing fee. Publication of this play does not imply availability for performance. Both amateurs and professionals considering a production are strongly advised to apply to the appropriate agent before starting rehearsals, advertising, or booking a theatre. A licensing fee must be paid whether the title is presented for charity or gain and whether or not admission is charged.

The professional rights in this play are controlled by Samuel French Ltd, 52 Fitzroy Street, London, W1T 5JR.

No one shall make any changes in this title for the purpose of production. No part of this book may be reproduced, stored in a retrieval system, or transmitted in any form, by any means, now known or yet to be invented, including mechanical, electronic, photocopying, recording, videotaping, or otherwise, without the prior written permission of the publisher. No one shall upload this title, or part of this title, to any social media websites.

The right of Robert Bloomfield to be identified as author of this work has been asserted in accordance with Section 77 of the Copyright, Designs and Patents Act 1988.

PORTRAIT OF MURDER

Produced by Bob Swash in association with Ben Kamsler at the Savoy Theatre, London, on the 24th October 1963, subsequently at the Vaudeville Theatre, London, with the following cast of characters:

(in the order of their appearance)

TOD LOGAN	*Tenniel Evans*
AGNES WEBSTER	*Barbara Hicks*
ELIOT BARLOW	*George Baker*
PAULA BARLOW	*Phyllis Calvert*
DENISE MURRAY	*Renee Asherson*
JAMES GUTHRIE	*Jack Gwillim*

Directed by GEORGE SHDANOFF

Setting by MALCOLM PRIDE

SYNOPSIS OF SCENES

The action of the Play passes in the living-room of the Barlows' house in Kent

ACT I

SCENE 1 A Monday morning in late August
SCENE 2 Afternoon, a week later
SCENE 3 Late afternoon the following day

ACT II

SCENE 1 The evening of the same day
SCENE 2 Later the same night

Time—the present

Facing page 1—Portrait of Murder

Photograph by Angus McBean

ACT I

Scene i

Scene—*The living-room of the Barlows' house in Kent. A Monday morning in late August.*

The house is a reconverted farmhouse, with a timbered ceiling and a large open brickwork fireplace R. *The upstage half of the room forms the hall and is dominated by a distinctive spiral staircase up* LC, *leading to the bedrooms. In the hall, the front door is off* R *and the kitchen* L, *and a glass door* C *gives access to the garden. In the room there is a row of built-in bookshelves* L, *a section of which is hinged, forming a door leading to the study. The room is furnished with pieces from various periods. Immediately above the fireplace is a long, sectioned, curved divan, and below the fireplace is an armchair with a pouffe* L *of it. A stool stands* L *of the divan. The whole forms a conversational group about a low coffee-table in front of the fireplace which dominates the right wall. A framed portrait of Paula Barlow hangs above the mantel. The painting depicts a handsome, poised woman in her thirties. Behind the divan is a bar on which there is a telephone. A writing-desk stands against the bookshelves* L, *with a high-backed swivel armchair* R *of it and a small upright chair below it. At night the room is lit by table-lamps on the bar and on the desk and a wall-bracket behind the bar. Books by Paula Winsten fill some of the shelves* L.

When the Curtain *rises, the stage is in darkness. Then a spotlight pinpoints the portrait of Paula in the darkness. An eerie musical theme sneaks in softly. Now, slowly, as the music builds, light sweeps the stage, disclosing the living-room, unoccupied for the moment. The music fades into the clatter of a typewriter in the study* L, *then fades out. The typing continues.* Tod Logan *enters up* C *from the garden, carrying a bouquet of white carnations.* Tod *is waspish, arrogant, carefully elegant; he seems marshmallow soft, like a petulant middle-aged baby. He goes off* L *in the hall for a moment, then re-enters holding a pile of unopened letters that he has collected from the front door. He moves* C, *pauses to listen to the typing and then snoops around the room before halting and cupping his hands to his mouth so that the bouquet resembles a megaphone.*

Tod (*yelling like an urchin*) Come out, come out, wherever you are.

(*The typing stops abruptly*)

Agnes (*off* L; *startled*) Yes? Who's there?

(Tod *exits quickly* L *in the hall.*
     Agnes Webster *enters* L *from the study, peering owlishly through horn-rimmed glasses. Nearing forty,* Agnes *still divides humanity into*

two classes, authors and other people. *Flustered by the interruption, she goes up* C, *looks outside into the garden, shakes her head in puzzlement, then turns back to the study.*

Tod *enters quickly and quietly up* L *and prods Agnes from behind with the bouquet stem*)

Tod. Boo! (*He moves* C)
Agnes (*spinning round*) Oh—Mr Logan! (*She stands with her back to the desk chair*)
Tod (*with a sweeping bow*) Agnes, my love.
Agnes. I'm afraid I didn't hear you ring.
Tod. You were banging away like billy-o, Miss Webster. (*He hands her the letters*) Here. More letters for you to answer. I picked them off the mat.
Agnes (*facing front*) Oh, all these letters! Sometimes I wonder if there's a country in the world where Mrs Barlow's books aren't read.
Tod (*moving* RC *and looking up at the portrait*) The publicity Eliot's got for Paula has really paid off, hasn't it?

(Agnes *moves* C)

(*Musingly*) Aggie, how does a best-selling novelist see her public? (*He looks over his shoulder at Agnes*) As an enormous pair of lips spelling out S-E-X?
Agnes. I wouldn't know, Mr Logan. I'm only a writer's secretary.
Tod (*moving to* R *of her*) Only a secretary? Don't be so modest, Aggie—you're a poet in your own right.
Agnes (*moving* LC; *embarrassed*) Oh, Mr Logan—please . . .
Tod. You know it's true. Now—(*he moves to* R *of her*) what are you writing these days? Let me hear your latest epic.
Agnes. It's nothing, really—(*she moves towards the study door*) just a tiny lyric.
Tod. Well, let's hear it, girl.
Agnes. I've only just begun it.
Tod. Agnes—recite. Them's orders.
Agnes. We-ell—if you insist. (*She takes a piece of typescript from her pocket, delicately clears her throat and reads*)
"Come back, my love—return, return!
Bring back the heart for which I yearn.
Forsake your wanton Jezebels—
Renounce their satins, gold and jewels . . ."
(*She looks up*) That's all—so far.
Tod. Aggie, I do hope it has a happy ending.
Agnes. But, Mr Logan, it's a poem.
Tod (*moving to* R *of her*) What does Eliot think about it?
Agnes. Mr Barlow? Oh, you're the first to hear this one.
Tod (*moving to the hall and looking around*) By the way, where is Eliot?

AGNES (*moving up* C; *awkwardly*) He—er—isn't here.

TOD. Well, he won't grieve over missing me. (*He hands the bouquet to Agnes*) My daily contribution, dear heart. (*He crosses to the fireplace*) Be sure Eliot takes them to Paula when he goes to the hospital. (*He studies the portrait with self-satisfaction*)

AGNES (*moving down* C; *ill at ease*) I'm sorry, Mr Logan. He won't be able to do that today.

TOD (*turning to her*) Damn! Not coming home before he visits Paula, eh?

AGNES (*turning away*) We-ell, no—not exactly.

TOD (*absently*) Not exactly? (*He pauses, then guesses the truth*) Aggie! Has Eliot gone to bring her home?

(AGNES *looks away*)

(*He moves to her*) Agnes Penelope, look at me.

(AGNES *reluctantly looks at Tod*)

Now—give me the low-down.

AGNES (*unhappily*) Mr Barlow wanted it kept secret.

TOD. Secret? From me?

AGNES. He doesn't want the newspaper and TV people to bother us. If they find out, they'll swoop down here like a pack of jackals.

TOD. You mean our boy isn't trying to get publicity for Paula? Isn't he feeling well?

AGNES. I don't make the arrangements in this house. I simply carry out orders.

TOD. Dearest Aggie, loyal and true. Well, don't forget to put those things in water. (*He looks at the portrait*) Paula will know she's home when she sees white carnations.

AGNES (*soberly*) I hope so. (*Nervously*) They'll be home shortly. I don't know whether you should be here.

TOD. Thank you, my love. (*He moves to the garden door*)

AGNES (*moving to him; contritely*) Oh, no offence, really. But the doctors have warned Mr Barlow. Her period of—well, readjustment —may be rather difficult.

TOD. Rest easy, love. Paula can always depend on me.

AGNES. Mr Logan—(*she looks away*) I didn't mean to offend you.

TOD. Agnes, it takes an expert to insult Tod Logan. Don't forget to put those flowers in water.

(TOD *exits* R *in the hall*.

AGNES *exits* L *in the hall to the kitchen. There is a pause.*

ELIOT BARLOW *and* PAULA *enter from the garden.* ELIOT *is personable, self-assured and charming. His manner toward Paula is attentive and gentle. He carries two suitcases.* PAULA *somehow seems younger and less poised than her portrait. She has a slightly defensive air, like a sensitive child in a strange and possibly hostile world, as she moves* C *and looks wonderingly about her.* ELIOT *puts the cases down up* RC *then moves to* L *of Paula*)

ELIOT (*gently*) Yes, Paula—this is where it happened. After the house caught fire from the explosion, Guthrie found you in here and pulled you outside. (*He takes Paula's coat and hangs it over the desk chair*) It's just as I told you. The entire house had to be rebuilt, and we searched everywhere to duplicate all the old pieces. This room looks exactly the way it was before your accident.

(PAULA *shivers*)

(*Quickly*) What's the matter, dear?
PAULA. I—I suddenly felt cold. Perhaps it's going to rain.
ELIOT (*lightly*) For your homecoming? Darling, it wouldn't dare.

(PAULA *moves to the fireplace, looks up and studies the portrait*)

PAULA. Eliot—you said my portrait was destroyed by the fire.
ELIOT (*moving to* L *of Paula*) I wanted to surprise you. Logan did this one from the photographs.
PAULA. Did I really look like this before my accident?
ELIOT. It's a perfect likeness.
PAULA. I'm different, now. (*She crosses to the desk chair*) I've changed.
ELIOT. Paula, everyone changes. We all get older—even in ten months. But you seem younger now in every way. (*He moves to* R *of Paula to touch her*)

(PAULA *withdraws*)

Paula—I'm your husband.
PAULA. I know. So Dr Kendall tells me—and Dr Schuyler—and you . . . (*She turns to him. Helplessly*) And yet—no matter what any of you say . . .
ELIOT. Am I still a stranger to you? Even here?
PAULA. I hoped I'd have a sense of belonging when I came home —but, instead . . . (*She moves up* L. *Frightened*) Eliot, you've got to help me. I don't remember this room. I don't remember anything at all.

(ELIOT *moves to* R *of Paula, puts his arm around her and leads her down* C)

ELIOT. You know what Dr Schuyler told you. Everyone feels lost in the dark—and yet daylight always comes.
PAULA. I don't even recognize myself.
ELIOT. You're Paula Barlow, my wife. You detested sentimentality, you wouldn't even wear a wedding ring—but I thought you might like this. (*He takes a small box from his pocket, extracts a diamond-set wedding ring and puts it on her finger*)
PAULA. Eliot, it's beautiful!

SCENE I — PORTRAIT OF MURDER

ELIOT. Welcome home, Mrs Barlow. (*He gently kisses her*)

(AGNES *enters from the hall carrying a vase filled with Tod's white carnations. She halts with surprise*)

AGNES. Oh—I'm sorry.

ELIOT (*moving up* RC) Oh, hello, Aggie. (*To Paula*) Darling, this is Agnes.

(AGNES *moves* LC. PAULA *faces Agnes with shy apprehension.* AGNES *returns her gaze guardedly, as if unsure of both herself and Paula*)

PAULA. I've heard all about you, Agnes—but I'm afraid I . . . (*Helplessly*) I'm sorry. I don't recognize you.

AGNES (*awkwardly*) Well—you haven't changed much, Mrs Barlow. I mean—after all you've been through—I didn't know what to expect. But you're home, now. That's the important thing—isn't it, Mr Barlow?

ELIOT. It is, indeed.

(AGNES *puts the vase on the bar*)

Tod Logan been here?

AGNES. Yes, he called with these.

ELIOT. When was that?

AGNES. Just a few minutes ago. (*To Paula*) I'm busy answering letters—but if you'd like some tea . . .

PAULA. No, thank you.

ELIOT (*with a step towards Agnes*) Later, Agnes. Why don't you take a breather, now?

AGNES. I—I think I will. (*She turns to go, then stops and turns to Paula*) You'll find all your things in order in your room, Mrs Barlow.

ELIOT (*moving up* C) I'll take your cases upstairs.

(ELIOT *exits* R *in the hall*. PAULA *and* AGNES *stand silent, then speak together*)

AGNES } (*together*) { Mrs Barlow——
PAULA }   { My husband tells me . . .
AGNES. —if there's anything at all I can do . . .

(*Both break off awkwardly. Then they smile, still strangers.*
ELIOT *enters* R *in the hall, carrying two suitcases, and exits upstairs*)

ELIOT (*ascending the stairs*) I left the typewriter for you, Agnes. Bring it up, will you?

AGNES (*hastily*) Oh, of course.

(AGNES *exits* R *in the hall.*
AGNES *enters* R *in the hall carrying a portable typewriter and exits with it up the stairs.* PAULA *sighs heavily, then sits on the divan and looks up at the portrait.*
TOD *enters quietly from the garden*)

Tod (*moving* c) Welcome home, my lovely—ten thousand welcomes.

(Paula *looks round sharply, startled, and stares at* Tod *without recognition. He in turn looks at her intently for a moment*)

Paula?

Paula (*rising*) Yes.

Tod (*studying her*) Hmmmmm! (*He raises his hands, rubs his fingers together and clucks pensively*) I don't know—have *I* changed, I wonder? Of course, I'm practically senile with anxiety about you by now.

Paula. I'm sorry. Who are you?

Tod (*with a Cyrano flourish*) Dearest love, I'm Tod Logan.

Paula. Oh, the flowers every day—the white carnations—and my portrait . . .

Tod. Worthy of Rembrandt—no?

Paula (*with a rueful smile*) I—I don't know.

Tod. Then you know nothing about me? Well, I'm a genius, like you. I make money at it, like you. I'm unbearable, unblushing, and unattached. I, too, live on this side of the river, so near that on a quiet day you can hear my cat sneeze. And I'm passionately loyal to my two greatest friends—you and me. Doesn't that ring the tiniest bell inside you?

(Paula *slowly shakes her head.*
Eliot *enters down the stairs*)

Eliot (*moving to* L *of Tod; annoyed*) I thought you'd gone, Logan.

Tod (*blandly*) When Agnes told me my favourite model was coming home today?

Eliot. She said you'd dropped in for just a minute.

Tod. Can't trust anyone nowadays, can you? (*To Paula*) They've changed you, dearest.

Paula. Agnes doesn't think I've changed.

Tod. Aggie's not an artist. No insight.

(Eliot *moves above the divan*)

(*Thoughtfully*) Somehow you're not the complex personality I remember—Paula Winsten, novelist—Paula Barlow, housewife, after a fashion . . .

Paula. Was I complex?

Tod. Oh, Paula!

Paula. I feel empty inside.

Eliot (*leaning over the back of the divan; gently*) Darling, you know we promised to go slowly and patiently. (*To Tod*) She doesn't appreciate the progress she's made. Ten months ago we thought only a miracle could save her. Now look at her—newer than new.

Tod (*to Paula*) Frankly, angel, from what Eliot told me—the extent of your injuries—I hardly hoped to recognize you.

Eliot. Thank God we had Kendall for our surgeon. What

might've taken two years, with his new techniques was done in half that time. Kendall had to use photographs of her. He had to rebuild the entire facial structure.
TOD (*to Paula*) Like me with your portrait, love.
PAULA. So Eliot told me. But don't look too closely. The scars are under my hairline.
TOD. Eliot said the vocal chords were damaged—the throat lining . . .
ELIOT. Yes. When I first began to visit her, when they finally let me see her, Paula couldn't speak at all.
PAULA. I was so frightened.
TOD. No need to be now.
PAULA (*with a sudden shiver*) I still wake up at night—on the verge of screaming. (*She crosses to the desk chair*) Then I lie in the dark, trying to remember how it happened, knowing I could've been scarred for life . . .
TOD (*moving to* R *of Paula*) Instead, you're beautiful. You can start life all over again, like a phoenix.
PAULA (*turning to Tod*) How can I start all over again when I don't remember what went before? You can't imagine what it means to stand here—like this—and not know who you are. Nothing's the same, now—not for any of us.
ELIOT (*crossing to her; soothingly*) Paula, it will be—I promise.

(*The front-door bell rings.* PAULA *starts nervously, and looks at Eliot*)

(*He moves up* C) I'll just answer the door.
PAULA (*crossing to* C) Eliot!

(ELIOT *stops and turns*)

I don't think I can face anybody else just now.
TOD. Don't hesitate to throw me out, Princess. I'm your slave, as always.
ELIOT. I'll see who it is.

(ELIOT *exits into the hall*)

PAULA. Oh, I don't mean you, Tod. But the idea of meeting too many people all at once—(*she gives a helpless gesture*) it—it terrifies me.

(TOD *moves to the desk and picks up a book*)

TOD (*reading the title*) *Weep for Adonais.* It's still your best book—or hasn't Eliot told you?
PAULA. All I know is what Eliot's told me. (*She moves to the fireplace. Reciting, as if by rote*) Except for Eliot, I've no family at all. I'd almost finished a new novel, just before my accident, but the manuscript was destroyed in the fire. And this is my house—where I did my writing . . .

Tod. You bought it after *Weep for Adonais* hit the jackpot. (*He replaces the book on the desk*) Before you met Eliot.
Paula. Who had a small part in a play someone adapted from my second novel—correct?
Tod. Perfect. (*He crosses to her*) Eliot was a promising young actor at the time. He'd been promising for a number of years. Then Paula Winsten became Paula Barlow, and Eliot found his career. He's been marvellous for you on contracts and getting you publicity.
Paula. Publicity's the last thing in the world I want just now.

(Denise Murray *enters from the hall.*
Eliot *follows her on.* Denise *is younger than Paula, under thirty, and is vivacious, impulsive, unpredictable, and really not very bright. She rushes forward delightedly when she sees Paula*)

Denise. Paula darling!

(Paula *steps back*)

How wonderful to see you!

(Denise *draws back, rebuffed by* Paula's *rigidity*)

Paula—don't you recognize me?
Tod. That should be obvious, my sweet—even to you.

(Denise *looks at Tod, then turns to Paula*)

Denise (*to Paula*) He hasn't changed, you know. Sweet as ever. (*She smiles*) I haven't changed, either. I'm Denise.
Paula (*with a slow, warm smile*) Oh—Denise. Hello.
Denise (*moving to the stool* c) I tried to come to the hospital—but Eliot was adamant about visitors. He even tried to keep me out just now.
Paula (*sitting on the left end of the divan*) Don't blame Eliot. I've been afraid to meet anyone new.
Denise. Afraid? (*She sits on the stool. Slowly*) You've changed, Paula. You've—really changed.
Tod. How did you know she was coming home today, my love? Agnes said it was a state secret.
Denise. Eliot told me when I phoned. I think I deserve that much as Paula's greatest friend.
Paula. Are you, Denise?

(Denise *stares blankly at Paula*)

Are you my greatest friend?
Denise (*recovering*) Paula, everyone knows how close we were. Don't you remember? (*She turns away; contritely*) Oh, I'm an idiot. I can't get it through my head . . .
Tod. Of course you're an idiot. But don't blame your stupidity this time. Even I find it hard to cope with Paula's amnesia.

ELIOT. We all have to get used to it. But we've agreed to go slowly and patiently, haven't we, dear?
PAULA. Yes, Eliot.
TOD (*crossing to the fireplace*) Well, I won't overstay my welcome. Paula dear—I'll drop in soon—if you don't object.

(DENISE *rises and moves* L)

Denise—I still need a throne chair for my Lady Dimsdell sitting. Something to match her delightful personality—mouldy—slightly wormy—falling apart here and there . . .
DENISE. You've seen everything I have in the shop, Tod.
TOD. Haven't you picked up any new monstrosities lately?
DENISE. Not a blessed thing.
TOD. Weren't you scouting an auction in Canterbury last week?
DENISE. Canterbury?
TOD. Someone mentioned seeing you—can't remember who, offhand. (*Lightly*) You see, Paula? You're not the only one with memory trouble. (*He moves up* C *to the hall and turns*) Take good care of your bride, Eliot. Don't let any more accidents happen to her.

(TOD *blows a kiss to Paula and exits to the hall*)

DENISE. If Tod's talent matched his ego, he wouldn't be Tod Logan. He'd be Michaelangelo. How do you like this room, Paula?
PAULA. I think it's charming.
DENISE. Eliot and I worked at it together—did he tell you? I'd decorated the house for you in the first place, so he asked me to redo it. We duplicated every single piece, including Paula Barlow's favourite chair. (*She indicates the desk chair*)
PAULA. Is that my favourite chair?
DENISE. You did all your writing here. Nobody dared use it—artistic temperament, you know.

(PAULA *rises and sways slightly*)

ELIOT (*moving quickly to Paula*) What's the matter, dear? (*He puts his arm around her*)
PAULA. I just feel shaky. It's the first time I've been up so long.
ELIOT. I'll take you to your room.

(PAULA *stiffens*)

I've moved my own things out. I thought you're prefer to be alone.
PAULA (*softly*) Thank you, Eliot.

(*The telephone rings.* PAULA *reacts nervously.* ELIOT *smiles reassuringly, goes to the bar and lifts the telephone receiver.* PAULA *crosses to* R *of Denise*)

ELIOT (*into the telephone*) Hello? . . . Yes, speaking . . . Put him on . . .

PAULA (*to Denise*) I do hope you'll excuse me. (*She collects her coat from the desk chair*)
DENISE. I should've phoned first. It was thoughtless of me.
PAULA. Please stay. Keep Eliot company.
ELIOT (*into the telephone*) Hello, Jim. I thought you were in Paris . . . Oh, just leaving . . . Well, the truth is, Paula's home . . . That's right . . . Just a moment . . . (*He covers the mouthpiece. To Paula*) Jim wants to say "hello', Paula.

(PAULA *begs off, almost tearfully*)

(*Into the telephone*) Jim? . . . She's awfully tired—she'll call you later on . . . What? . . .
DENISE. Paula, I hope you remember Jim. A writer can't afford to forget her agent.
PAULA. Especially when he saved my life.
ELIOT (*into the telephone*) They did? . . . How much? . . . Is that all? . . . Well, all right—do the best you can . . . So long. (*He replaces the receiver*) Jim sends his love. He's jetting over to Paris on business. He says a cable came from Hollywood today. (*To Denise*) There's interest in a story Paula wrote three years ago.
DENISE. Paula, how wonderful!
PAULA. I'll leave everything to you, Eliot. May I go to my room?
ELIOT. I'll take you.
PAULA. No! No! Please. Just tell me. I'll have to learn my own way around.
ELIOT. At least let Agnes help you. (*He goes to the stairs and calls*) Oh, Agnes.
PAULA (*turning to Denise*) Thank you for coming, Denise. I'll have to learn to be friends all over again. Perhaps you can help me remember.
DENISE. Of course. (*She smiles*)

(AGNES *enters on the stairs*)

ELIOT. Agnes—show my wife to her room, will you?
AGNES. Of course, Mr Barlow.

(AGNES *exits up the stairs.*
PAULA *follows her off.* ELIOT *looks after Paula for a moment, then takes out a cigar and lights it*)

DENISE (*crossing to the fireplace*) She's different, isn't she?
ELIOT. I told you she was.
DENISE. I don't mean her looks. (*Thoughtfully*) She said she was afraid to meet anyone new. I never thought I'd hear Paula Barlow admit she was afraid of anything.
ELIOT (*moving down* RC; *musingly*) Guthrie says he can get twenty thousand for those film rights. He ought to get thirty.
DENISE. When did you give her the ring?

ELIOT. Mmmmmm?
DENISE. Her wedding ring.
ELIOT (*amused; gently*) Denise, it's expected of me. I'm her husband.
DENISE. You don't have to remind me.
ELIOT. I thought I told you to stay away until next week?
DENISE. I couldn't wait to see what Paula looks like. And I haven't seen you since Canterbury.
ELIOT (*moving to Denise*) We'd better be careful now she's home.
DENISE (*turning away*) We've always been careful.
ELIOT. I'm afraid we haven't.
DENISE (*defensively*) How could I know Tod would find out I was in Canterbury last week?
ELIOT. It was a mistake to look in on that auction before joining me at the hotel.
DENISE. I know. (*Apprehensively*) You think Lady Dimsdell—or one of Tod's other crows—was there and saw me? It couldn't have been Tod, could it?
ELIOT. I'm not worried about Logan.
DENISE. These last few months have been so wonderful. Why must it all go wrong? (*She embraces Eliot*)
ELIOT. Denise, there was nothing wrong in my plan. I told you that the gas boiler would explode at exactly five forty-nine—and it did. Not a scrap of evidence to show I'd tampered with anything. Unfortunately, I had no control over outside factors. How could I know Jim Guthrie would blunder in and rescue Paula at the last moment?
DENISE. She's not the way you said she was at all, is she? (*Accusingly*) And you're still married to her—and all this still belongs to Paula.
ELIOT. Yes, for the time being.
DENISE. Eliot, how much longer must we wait?
ELIOT. Not long. I'll do it this time—without any mistake.

The LIGHTS BLACK-OUT

SCENE 2

SCENE—*The same. Afternoon. A week later.*
When the CURTAIN *rises, it is a sunny afternoon.* ELIOT *is standing at the bar.* JAMES GUTHRIE *is sitting on the divan, at the right end of it. He is a big man, fortyish and outwardly gruff. Neither* JAMES *nor* ELIOT *has any use for the other, but they hide it well.*

ELIOT (*pouring two drinks*) And how was Paris this time, Jim?
GUTHRIE. Oh, the usual mixture. Too much cognac—not enough

sleep—and nothing to justify my trip as a tax deduction. This year's crop of French writers loses a great deal in translation.

ELIOT (*smiling*) You say that every year. (*He hands a drink to Guthrie*) Cheers. (*He moves to the stairs*)

GUTHRIE. Cheers.

(*They drink*)

Eliot—explain this film offer to Paula right away, won't you? I've promised to get back to them in California by tomorrow.

ELIOT (*looking up the stairs*) I'll tell her as soon as she wakes up. Is twenty thousand the best you could do?

GUTHRIE. Impossible to get any higher. In any case, it may help compensate for the novel that went up in smoke.

(*The sound of typing comes from the study* L)

ELIOT. Don't expect Paula to react one way or the other. She's completely indifferent to losing all that work.

GUTHRIE. That doesn't sound like Paula.

ELIOT. Well, frankly, Jim . . . (*He breaks off, goes to the study door and calls*) Agnes, if you don't mind . . .

(*The typing ceases*)

(*He closes the study door, crosses and sits* L *of Guthrie on the divan*) When that gas boiler exploded last November, it blew my marriage to hell. Paula and I are strangers now. Complete and utter strangers.

GUTHRIE. Eliot, I can only tell you what I've said before. You've had seven years together. It's up to you to help her remember what you've shared.

ELIOT. It isn't that easy.

GUTHRIE. Nothing's easy. But as long as you know she'll regain her memory in the long run . . .

ELIOT. Eventually. But at the moment, everything she experienced before the explosion is completely wiped out.

GUTHRIE. Completely? The last time we talked, you said she'd suffered only partial brain damage.

ELIOT. Her head injuries destroyed certain of the brain cells that store up memory. But the doctors say that Paula's basic trouble is functional amnesia not organic. There's some kind of mental or emotional block, like a locked door between her and the past.

GUTHRIE. You mean Paula doesn't want to remember? (*Pause*) I see . . . What about her writing? Anything new there?

ELIOT. I took a typewriter to her in the hospital last month. It was still in its case when she came home.

GUTHRIE. I wish I could help you, Eliot. I'd like to help both of you. But in a case like this . . . (*He shrugs helplessly. Thoughtfully*) How about Denise?

(PAULA *enters slowly down the stairs*)

ELIOT (*on guard*) What?
GUTHRIE. She and Paula were always great friends. Can't Denise help?
ELIOT. I'm afraid not. (*He rises*) Let me get you another drink, Jim.

(PAULA *reaches the foot of the stairs*)

(*He sees Paula*) Paula! (*He moves* R *of her*) Jim Guthrie's here.

(GUTHRIE *rises*. PAULA *turns with new interest and crosses silently to* L *of Guthrie*. GUTHRIE *eyes* PAULA *appraisingly, matching her own guarded scrutiny, then he smiles and extends his hand*)

GUTHRIE. Hello, Paula.
PAULA. So you're Jim. (*She shakes hands*) I'm delighted to meet you—Jim. Eliot, why didn't you let me know he was here?
GUTHRIE (*moving to the fireplace*) Don't blame your husband. He said you were sleeping. I told him not to disturb you.
PAULA. I'm not that fragile. (*She sits* C *of the divan*) And I've been wanting to see you.
GUTHRIE. I should hope so. I've contracts galore for you to sign—reprints and translations—TV adaptations of your short stories... (*He sits* R *of Paula on the divan*)
PAULA. I wasn't thinking of business. I wanted to thank you for saving my life.
GUTHRIE. Pure luck. Another minute and I'd have been too late.
PAULA. You might've been killed.
ELIOT (*sitting on the stool* C) An agent? Only ten per cent of him.
GUTHRIE. Your husband's still an actor at heart, Paula.
PAULA. Eliot tells me you were in hospital yourself for a month.
GUTHRIE (*shrugging*) A few scars here and there. Underneath I'm still the old Guthrie. Not new, like you.
PAULA. Not exactly new—just remodelled. Now I've got to remember everything I've forgotten.
ELIOT. I keep on telling her we've got to go slowly.
GUTHRIE. Your husband and I don't always agree, Paula, but he's right this time. (*He pauses briefly*) I drove down from London about that film offer, you know.
PAULA. I thought Eliot was going to discuss it with you.
GUTHRIE. The story's your property. You have to sign the contracts.
PAULA. I can't just yet.
ELIOT. I still think we ought to get more than twenty thousand—but I'll take it.
GUTHRIE. Is that acceptable to you, Paula?
PAULA. Oh, yes. Anything Eliot says.
GUTHRIE. All right. But I still want to bring you up to date on your affairs. When can we do that?
PAULA. Not yet. Later.

GUTHRIE (*rising*) Your publisher wants to see you. Why don't you come up to London next week and have lunch with George Waller and me? We'll pick a quiet spot. No-one will recognize you.

PAULA. Oh, no. I'd rather you came here, Jim. (*Helplessly*) Everything outside this house frightens me. It's all so overwhelming and mysterious.

GUTHRIE (*bending down to her*) Paula, you've fought for what you want all your life—you can't give up, now.

PAULA. You sound like Dr Schuyler.

GUTHRIE. Well, good-bye. (*He moves up* C) And don't forget—I'm looking forward to that next book. (*To Eliot*) I'll be in touch, Eliot.

ELIOT (*rising and moving to Guthrie*) Oh, Jim—could you give me a lift to the village? I want to pick up my car at the garage.

GUTHRIE. No trouble at all. Good-bye, Paula.

(GUTHRIE *exits into the hall*)

ELIOT (*moving to* L *of the divan*) I won't be long, darling. You don't mind being left alone?

PAULA. Alone? Isn't Agnes here?

ELIOT. Aggie? (*He points to the study door*) Busy with your correspondence.

(ELIOT *kisses Paula lightly, then exits into the hall.* PAULA *rises, crosses to the study door, opens it and stands in the doorway*)

AGNES (*off*) Mrs Barlow! Is there anything I can do for you?

PAULA. Yes, there is. (*She turns and moves* C)

(AGNES *enters from the study, peering quizzically through her glasses. She has a letter in her hand*)

AGNES. Yes?

PAULA. Come in, Agnes. Sit down, please.

(AGNES *crosses to the divan and sits*)

Sit down and talk to me.

AGNES. Talk to you? (*Uncomfortably*) I—I'm still behind on your letters. This one, for instance—from Dover. One of your readers. Really devoted to you—like so many others. Named Irene Morgan. She writes regularly enquiring after your health.

PAULA. That's very sweet. But you can answer it later.

AGNES. In the old days, you always answered immediately.

PAULA (*crossing to the armchair* R) Agnes, I've been home a week now. How often have we talked together in that time?

AGNES (*lamely*) Well, I—I've been busy. Mr Barlow told me to send out printed letters about your accident. But in all fairness to your readers I prefer to do them individually. It all takes time.

PAULA (*sitting in the armchair* R) I'd hoped we'd be friends.

AGNES. Friends?

PAULA. Is that so unusual?
AGNES. Oh, no. But I—well, I—I'll have to get used to it. We never really talked much in the old days.
PAULA. Why not?
AGNES. We were always busy. And your free time took you up to London—for interviews, autographing parties, conferences with your publisher and Mr Guthrie. Don't you remember?
PAULA (*burying her head in her hands*) I remember nothing—nothing. (*She looks up*) Please. Talk to me. Tell me all you know about me.
AGNES (*still resisting*) What can I say that Mr Barlow hasn't already told you?
PAULA. Do you know what he's told me? The places we've visited—Nice, Capri—my migraine headaches—how we met when someone dramatized my second novel . . .
AGNES. Yes, he played "Tony Goodwin" in *Bright Midnight*. I never thought the play did justice to your characters.
PAULA. I've seen the reviews in the scrap-books George Waller sent me. Eliot was barely mentioned.
AGNES. It wasn't a very big part. (*Awkwardly*) Mrs Barlow—if you've gone through your scrap-books—and if you've read your novels . . .
PAULA. I've read every word I've ever published. It doesn't help me.

(AGNES *is silent*)

(*Anguished*) Last night I woke in the dark. I was afraid, like a child. Afraid of everything I don't know and can't remember. My husband was sleeping in the next room—and yet I couldn't call out. He's a stranger to me, like everyone else.

(*Soft music is heard*)

AGNES (*after a pause*) What do you want to know, Mrs Barlow?
PAULA. What happened the day of the fire? The day my old life ended.

(*The* LIGHTS *start to dim*)

AGNES. We-ell—you slept late, as usual. I typed up your dictation from the day before. Then I took breakfast up to you in bed. Nothing elaborate—just toast and coffee. And the new pages.
PAULA. Was that a regular routine?
AGNES. More or less. I often made breakfast and lunch. You and Mr Barlow usually went out for dinner. You didn't care for servants in the house. (*She rises*)
PAULA (*rising and moving up* L) Strange about sleeping late. Now I wake before six every morning.

(*The* LIGHTS BLACK-OUT.

PAULA *and* AGNES *exit up* L *in the* BLACK-OUT.
ELIOT *enters in the* BLACK-OUT, *goes to the telephone and lifts the receiver*)

AGNES (*off*) I was rather tired that day. You see, we'd worked quite hard the previous day. When I came downstairs, I could hear Mr Barlow on the phone, here in the living-room.

(*The* LIGHTS *come up*)

ELIOT (*into the telephone*) Look here, I don't want to argue . . .

(AGNES *down the stairs*)

We can't discuss it on the phone . . . I'll tell you what I'll do. It's nine-thirty now—I'll leave for London. How does that strike you? . . . We'll discuss everything when we meet . . .

(*The music fades*)

I'm counting on you. Good-bye. (*He replaces the receiver and turns to* Agnes) Oh, Agnes. How's the barometer this morning?

AGNES. Could be stormy. She'll have a migraine attack if she doesn't take her caffeine pills.

ELIOT (*pouring himself a drink*) Agnes, no! When I got in from London last night, she was in high spirits.

AGNES. I know. She dictated twenty pages yesterday.

ELIOT. So, if she runs true to form, she'll have a let-down today. (*He glances at his watch*) Well, I'm afraid I can't help. I have a business appointment in town again.

AGNES. I'll be leaving soon myself. I'm driving down to Brighton.

ELIOT. Oh, really? Anything up?

AGNES. I told you—my niece is nine years old today. I'm helping my sister with young Deborah's party.

ELIOT. Well, hurray for Deborah. (*He takes out his wallet*) Here's something to help the tiddler celebrate. (*He hands Agnes a bank-note*)

AGNES. Oh, thank you, Mr Barlow.

ELIOT. Tell Paula I'll be back this evening. I'll call her if I'm going to be late. (*He moves up* C) Whoop it up at the party, Agnes. And kiss Debby for me.

AGNES. I will, indeed. Good-bye.

(ELIOT *exits into the hall.* AGNES *looks after him for a moment, looks up the stairs, then crosses to the bar and pours some soda-water for herself. She sips the drink, puts the glass on the coffee-table, sits on the divan, takes a piece of paper and pencil from her pocket and starts writing.*

MRS BARLOW, *unseen by* AGNES, *enters quietly down the stairs, smoking a cigarette and carrying some typescript. This is the* MRS BARLOW *of the portrait, now wearing a peignoir and in a foul mood. She moves* LC)

MRS BARLOW (*with her back to* Agnes; *caustically*) Busy slaving, Agnes?

SCENE 2   PORTRAIT OF MURDER   17

(AGNES, *startled, hastily stuffs the clipping in her pocket and rises*)

AGNES. Mrs Barlow! I—I didn't think you'd finished breakfast so quickly.

MRS BARLOW (*turning*) Did you expect me to start on it? What did you use for coffee? Instant mud?

AGNES. I'm sorry. I'll make a fresh pot. (*She moves up* C)

MRS BARLOW. Don't bother. My stomach will be happier if I just help you finish the gin. Or do you prefer Scotch in the morning?

AGNES (*with stiff dignity*) Mrs Barlow, you know I don't drink—at any hour of the day or night. (*She picks up her glass*) This is soda-water—for my digestion.

MRS BARLOW. So I was right about the coffee.

(AGNES *puts her glass on the bar and moves to the stairs*)

Where are you going?

AGNES. I'll bring down your breakfast tray.

MRS BARLOW. You can do that later. (*She stubs out her cigarette in the ashtray on the desk*) Where's Eliot?

AGNES. Mr Barlow had to go up to London.

MRS BARLOW. Again? Without telling me?

AGNES. He didn't want to bother you. He only just left.

MRS BARLOW. What's this trip for?

AGNES. He was on the phone about it, but I don't know who it was.

MRS BARLOW. You mean you've given up eavesdropping for Lent?

AGNES (*hurt*) Mrs Barlow!

MRS BARLOW. Oh, my error. A paragon of virtue, aren't you, dear? Saint Agnes, the Perfect. I didn't mean to wound your poetic soul.

AGNES. Mrs Barlow . . .

MRS BARLOW. Come now, Agnes. No-one keeps any secrets from me. I know all about your poetical fancies. How does your latest go? (*She quotes maliciously*)
  "The leaves of Autumn, like inky tears,
  Write sad love letters in the sky.
  Dropping there—dropping here . . ."

AGNES (*correcting her*) "Drifting here . . ."

MRS BARLOW (*acidly*) Oh—must be perfect, mustn't we? You might try applying your perfection to your spelling.

AGNES (*bewildered*) What's wrong with my spelling?

MRS BARLOW (*gesturing with the typescript*) How many "I's" in "aluminium"?

AGNES (*taking the typescript*) You told me to spell it that way. "Aluminum" you said—"because Sally Ann is an American." I have it in my shorthand book.

MRS BARLOW (*snatching the typescript*) Never mind. (*She crosses to the fireplace*) Do it again. (*She presses her hands to her temples*) My God, my God—I squeeze my brain dry day after day—and for what? I'm just a money-making machine for Eliot—Jim Guthrie—all the rest of you.

(Agnes *looks in silence at Mrs Barlow for a moment then turns to the stairs*)

(*Harshly*) Where do you think you're going?
AGNES (*tight-lipped*) I'll get your tray. I want to leave by twelve.
MRS BARLOW. Leave?
AGNES. I told Mr Barlow. I'm driving to Brighton.
MRS BARLOW. I've got a splitting headache. You can't leave me today.
AGNES. But you've known about my niece's birthday party for a week.
MRS BARLOW (*crossing to the desk chair*) You know what those migraines do to me. You can run the bath for me. Then you can rub my neck.
AGNES. I won't have time for that.
MRS BARLOW. Agnes, I said run my bath.
AGNES (*moving* C; *stubbornly*) I'm sorry. I've always given in to you —but I promised my niece I'd be there today.
MRS BARLOW (*moving to* L *of Agnes*) Isn't loyalty in your vocabulary? Or don't you care about your job?
AGNES. Don't threaten me, Mrs Barlow. I may not be a poet— but I'm not your slave—or your publisher, either. And don't talk to me about loyalty. You've had my loyalty for all these years—but when did you ever show me any consideration?

(*Soft music is heard*)

Run your own bath—and while you're at it, soak your bloody head in it.

(AGNES *exits* L *in the hall. The* LIGHTS *start to dim.* MRS BARLOW *moves wrathfully up* C *and looks off* L)

MRS BARLOW (*screaming*) Agnes! Agnes—come back here! (*Beside herself*) If you leave me now—don't ever come back! You hear me? And don't expect any references from me!

(*The* LIGHTS BLACK-OUT. *The music comes up strongly.*
MRS BARLOW *exits in the* BLACK-OUT.
AGNES *and* PAULA *enter in the* BLACK-OUT *and take up their previous positions,* AGNES *seated on the divan and* PAULA R *of the desk chair. The* LIGHTS *come up. The music fades*)

AGNES (*after a pause; unhappily*) I didn't want to tell you. You insisted on knowing the truth.
PAULA. Was that particular day unusual? Or was I always like that?

AGNES. Mrs Barlow—anyone who suffers from migraine . . .
PAULA. You've told me this much. (*She crosses to the armchair* R) I might as well know everything. Was that how I usually behaved?
AGNES (*reluctantly*) We-ell—you weren't the easiest person to get along with.
PAULA. You mean, I treated Eliot just as callously and brutally?
AGNES. It depended on how you felt. But Mr Barlow and I understood your moods. And he was devoted to you—just as he is now.

(PAULA *turns and looks at the portrait*)

PAULA (*slowly*) You went to Brighton that day?
AGNES. Oh, yes. I didn't tell anyone what had happened—but I swore I'd never work for you again.
PAULA (*turning to Agnes*) Why were you here when I came home? (*She sits* R *of Agnes on the divan*)
AGNES. Because Mr Barlow called me about the fire that night. I felt so guilty. After all, if I hadn't deserted you . . .
PAULA. You might've been burned—or even killed.
AGNES (*looking at Paula*) Or I might've noticed the gas boiler was leaking. Mr Barlow had suggested you have it looked at.
PAULA. Have you any idea who phoned Eliot that morning?
AGNES. None. But I've sometimes wondered whether *you* might've known. You *could've* listened in on your bedroom extension.

(*The front-door bell rings*)

(*She rises*) Excuse me.

(AGNES *exits into the hall. There is a brief pause.*
DENISE *enters from the hall. She is bright and cheerful*)

DENISE. Hello, Paula. (*She moves* C)
PAULA (*rising*) Denise . . .
DENISE. I arrived two steps behind a delivery van. Agnes is signing for the package, now.
PAULA. Oh, I see.
DENISE (*crossing and sitting in the armchair* R) I hope you don't mind my dropping in unannounced?
PAULA (*sitting on the divan*) No, of course not.

(*There is a pause*)

DENISE (*curious*) Anything the matter, dear?
PAULA. Oh, no. I'm all right.
DENISE (*looking away; casually*) Where's Eliot?
PAULA. Jim Guthrie gave him a lift into the village. He wanted to pick up his car at the garage.
DENISE. So you've finally met Jim?
PAULA. Yes.

(AGNES *enters from the hall, carrying a package*)

AGNES. For you, Mrs Barlow. (*She puts the package on the coffee-table*) I'll be in my room if you need me.

PAULA (*rising and moving* C) Thank you, Agnes.

(AGNES *exits into the hall*)

DENISE (*rising*) You haven't been on one of your old shopping sprees, have you, Paula?

PAULA (*bewildered*) I haven't stirred from the house. (*She moves to the coffee-table*) Help me, please.

(*They open the package.* DENISE *takes out a filmy nightdress*)

DENISE. Well!

PAULA (*taking the nightdress*) I feel like a—a kept woman.

DENISE. You're easily satisfied, dear. (*Casually*) Has Tod been back to bother you?

PAULA. No, I haven't seen or heard from him.

DENISE. Haven't you seen anybody at all?

PAULA. Nobody except Jim Guthrie.

DENISE. What do you think of Jim?

PAULA (*putting the nightdress on the coffee-table*) I like him. He seems dependable. (*She moves* C *and looks away*) What was our relationship like in the old days, Denise?

DENISE. Why, we were friends, of course.

PAULA (*turning to her*) Not us. Jim Guthrie and myself.

DENISE. Oh, Jim. (*She sits on the divan*) Jim's been your agent for years. You sent your first novel to him—after you picked his name from the telephone book.

PAULA. Yes, Eliot's told me about that. But he's never really said anything about Jim.

DENISE (*moving along the divan seat to the left end of it*) Don't you know why, darling? Oh, but of course you don't.

PAULA. Know why?

DENISE. Before Eliot came along, you were on the verge of marrying Jim.

PAULA (*surprised*) You mean I was in love with him?

DENISE. Let's say Jim was in love with you.

(PAULA *turns away*)

Then, I gather, Eliot took over. I don't suppose you've noticed it, but they loathe one another.

(PAULA *shakes her head*)

Did I speak out of turn, Paula?

PAULA. No, no. (*She pauses briefly*) Denise—you say we were friends?

DENISE. We still are.

PAULA (*turning to her*) Then I know I can trust you. What was I like before I lost my memory?

DENISE (*guardedly*) That's hard to say. We accept our friends as they are.

(PAULA *crosses to the fireplace and stands with her back to Denise*)

PAULA. Was I generous or considerate? Or was I possessive, suspicious, demanding . . . ?

DENISE (*lightly*) Oh, now, Paula. None of us is one of two extremes.

(ELIOT *enters* R *in the hall*)

You weren't a saint, but you weren't a hellcat, either. The truth is, dear . . .

ELIOT (*breaking in, moving* C; *to Paula*) Hello, darling. (*To Denise; casual and friendly*) Denise . . .

DENISE. Hello, Eliot.

ELIOT. Well, my car's in shape again, Paula—until next time. I see you've been busy.

DENISE (*pointedly*) Not as busy as you—or doesn't Paula have you to thank, Eliot?

ELIOT (*lightly*) You didn't think Agnes was responsible, did you?

DENISE. No—but there's always Jim Guthrie.

ELIOT (*moving to Paula and holding the nightdress up to her*) Like it, darling?

PAULA. I love it. Though it's hardly my style—or is it? (*Abruptly*) Excuse me. (*She crosses below Eliot and moves up* C)

ELIOT. I'm sorry, dear. (*He puts the nightdress on the coffee-table and follows Paula up* C) Let me help you.

PAULA. No, no. It's all right.

DENISE (*rising*) It's really my fault. I shouldn't have barged in on you without warning.

PAULA. Nonsense, Denise! Stay and talk to Eliot. I promise to be better company next time.

(PAULA *exits to the garden. Left alone,* DENISE *and* ELIOT *are silent as* ELIOT *looks after Paula.* DENISE *breaks the silence, tight-lipped with jealousy*)

DENISE. You're very loving with her.

ELIOT (*moving* LC; *amused*) Do you expect me to beat her?

DENISE. Hasn't she needed a nightgown until now? Or do you still have separate bedrooms?

ELIOT. You child! (*He crosses to her*) There's no need for this.

DENISE. Really? Is that why you've been avoiding me ever since you brought her home?

ELIOT. Denise—while she was in the hospital, I had time for you. But it's different now she's home.

DENISE (*crossing below Eliot to* LC; *bitterly*) Yes, very different.

ELIOT (*moving to the fireplace*) We can't risk any gossip. We have got to be careful.

DENISE. I'm sick and tired of being careful—and I'm tired of waiting.

ELIOT (*crossing to her*) Darling, darling—you think it's any easier for me? (*He puts his arms about her*) It's you I'm thinking of—your future—your safety—I won't move until I know there's no risk involved for you.

(DENISE *succumbs, as she always does, and enbraces him*)

DENISE. Oh, Eliot—I love you so much.

ELIOT (*softly*) Yes—yes, dear.

DENISE (*like a spoilt child*) Why can't we have everything the way we want it?

ELIOT. We will—but Paula's different, now.

DENISE. You mean she likes sexy nightgowns, now? Paula couldn't have changed that much. Your human iceberg—or do I misquote you? (*Reminiscently*) Have you forgotten our first time? I tried to hold you off—I really did—but you said, "Paula won't be back from London for hours." You said, "All her sex goes into her writing. It's like being married to a dictaphone." (*Low and coaxing*) You don't know what it means to keep me waiting this way.

ELIOT. I'll make it all up to you. Just be patient.

DENISE (*breaking from him to* LC) Patient! (*Naggingly*) Have you forgotten what it means to be her husband?

ELIOT. How can I forget the old Paula? Wherever we went, I had to lag two steps behind. (*He moves to the bar*) After all, I'm not a great writer—a big celebrity—just Paula Winsten's husband. At a restaurant or a night-club, my table was always in her name. And money! After all I did for her, not even a bank account of my own. She signed all the cheques, and tipped me like a servant. I'll never forget that.

DENISE. I was beginning to think you had forgotten.

ELIOT (*moving to her*) She's different now. She's changed.

DENISE (*looking away*) Well, I haven't changed. I still like nice things—and I know what to do with them.

ELIOT. I know you do. You'll get everything you deserve—in good time. (*He moves above the divan*)

DENISE. Don't wait too long, Eliot. (*She moves to him*) Eliot, you warned me Paula wasn't the same—she was ill—but don't be too sure about her.

ELIOT (*frowning*) Now what are you up to?

DENISE. Not me—Paula. She's up to her old tricks—playing games with you.

ELIOT. What kind of games?

DENISE. She's faking, Eliot. She remembers a lot more than you realize.

ELIOT (*leading her down* LC) No, Denise. The doctors tell me Paula may regain her memory eventually—but not now.

DENISE. She's faking, I tell you.

ELIOT. No, Denise, impossible.

DENISE. She knows I saw her the day of the fire. Nobody could tell her that. She was all alone when I came here that afternoon.

ELIOT (*slowly*) Denise, if you're lying to me . . .

DENISE (*losing control*) Don't you see? You've got to do something—before she remembers everything. Do something, Eliot—do something. (*She looks away*) Because if you don't . . .

ELIOT. Yes?

DENISE. I'll go to the police and tell them everything I know.

ELIOT. I see.

DENISE. They'd arrest you, Eliot. They'd find you guilty of attempted murder and send you to prison.

ELIOT. And what would happen to you while all this is happening to me?

DENISE. I don't care what happens to me. Everything would come out about the cheques you've forged—the things you've done with her securities—I'd be forced to testify against you.

ELIOT (*gently*) Denise—Denise—stop it.

DENISE (*turning to him*) I mean it, Eliot. If I can't have you all to myself—no Paula, nobody else at all, just the two of us . . .

ELIOT. What will you do? (*He takes her by the shoulders*) Pull the roof down on us—destroy the two of us?

DENISE. If I have to—yes.

(ELIOT *studies her thoughtfully*)

(*Tearfully*) Only because I love you. (*She embraces him*)

ELIOT (*softly*) Darling. (*He holds her close*) Trust me—a little longer. That isn't much to ask, is it?

DENISE. No.

ELIOT. All right, then. (*He pauses briefly*) You'd better get along now.

DENISE. Will you do it?

ELIOT. When I find the right way—the safe way. (*He pushes her away*) Now run along.

(DENISE *exits* R *in the hall*)

(*He ponders their exchange, troubled and irritated, then goes to the garden door and calls*) Paula! Paula! Why don't you come in, now?

(PAULA *enters from the garden and moves below the coffee-table*)

Denise has gone. She asked me to say good-bye for her.

PAULA. I'm sorry I was so silly.

ELIOT. Darling, does she depress you? She's such an adolescent.

PAULA. I thought you liked her.

ELIOT. She's young. She's no Paula Barlow. I'll tell her not to come if she disturbs you.

PAULA. No, Eliot, no.

ELIOT. What's troubling you, Paula?

PAULA. I made Agnes talk to me earlier.
ELIOT. What did Aggie tell you?
PAULA. That I was a selfish, hysterical hypochondriac.
ELIOT. Agnes said that?
PAULA. I don't like what I was.
ELIOT. You must have misunderstood her.
PAULA. No. She said you were always devoted to me. But I can't help wondering . . . There must have been times when you hated me.
ELIOT. Paula!
PAULA. I mean it.
ELIOT (*moving across to her*) Darling, no marriage is perfect. When we married, I had to make a choice between you and my career. I gave up my acting to devote my life to you, and I've never regretted a moment of it.
PAULA. It couldn't have been much fun for you these past months—day after day at the hospital—coping with my moods, my depressions.
ELIOT. Darling, I'm your husband. We're together, now—nothing else matters. I want to help you get well, Paula. I want to protect you.
PAULA. I know. (*She embraces him*) I feel safe with you, Eliot.
ELIOT. You are, darling. You are.

The LIGHTS BLACK-OUT

SCENE 3

SCENE—*The same. Late afternoon the following day.*

When the LIGHTS *come up, the room is empty. A fairly large cardboard carton containing a TV set is on the coffee-table. After a moment,* ELIOT *enters from the hall and crosses to the study door.*

ELIOT (*calling into the study*) Agnes, have you done those letters? (*He moves* LC)

    (AGNES *enters from the study, carrying a handful of letters to post. She has a shoulder-bag over her shoulder*)

AGNES. Yes, they're on the desk.
ELIOT. I've just come back from the hospital. I've been to see Dr Schuyler.
AGNES (*worried*) She's going to be all right, isn't she?
ELIOT. Nothing's changed. Paula's still the same.
AGNES. I'm sorry. I know how hard it is for you. But in the long run everything will come out right. Time is the great healer.
ELIOT. You ought to write a book yourself.
AGNES. Oh, not me. My little poems are my contribution. But

SCENE 3   PORTRAIT OF MURDER   25

one of these days Mrs Barlow will start writing again. And bit by bit, though it may take time, her memory will come back to her.
ELIOT. Where's Paula now? Sleeping?
AGNES. No—taking a bath. (*Earnestly*) I suppose we should be grateful she can't remember the actual explosion and the fire. Thank goodness she's been spared reliving that agony. But I often blame myself for not being here when it happened. (*Ingenuously*) I imagine you feel the same way.
ELIOT. Yes, Agnes, I do. I hope you haven't said anything else to distress her.
AGNES. I hope not, Mr Barlow. I didn't want to say anything to her yesterday, but she made me talk to her.
ELIOT. We'll have to be careful from now on.
AGNES. You know I will. By the way—Mr Guthrie's office called. He has the contracts from California. He's bringing them here later this afternoon.
ELIOT (*on edge*) I see. (*He turns away* R *and sees the carton*) Hello? What's this?
AGNES. Oh, that came just now. I thought it was something you ordered for Mrs Barlow.
ELIOT. Nothing to do with me. (*He lifts the carton for a moment*) It's heavy.
AGNES. Yes, I almost dropped it.
ELIOT. The label's smudged. It's either for Paula or for me. Shall we open it, Aggie?
AGNES. Yes, let's.

(ELIOT *opens the carton, takes out a portable TV set and puts it on the coffee-table*)

Why, it's a television set.
ELIOT (*taking out a card*) Here's the card. It's from Jim Guthrie.
AGNES. What a marvellous surprise.
ELIOT. When Jim drove me into the village yesterday, I told him how much television had helped Paula in hospital. I didn't expect him to do this. It's one of those new portables.
AGNES. Just imagine making them that small.
ELIOT. If they make them any smaller, we'll be wearing them on our wrists, like comic book astronauts.
AGNES (*shyly*) As a matter of fact, I've been tinkering with a little poem about television and our electronic age . . .
ELIOT. I think I remember. You sent it to *The Times Literary Supplement*.
AGNES. No, no, no. *Woman's Realm*. And it was about outer space. (*She clasps her hands and quotes*)
   "So high, my love, on yonder planet Arcturus—
   So far from earth, so far from me—
   What will meet you? Man or urus?"
ELIOT. "Urus"?

AGNES. It's an extinct wild ox. Not many people know about it, but how many words actually rhyme with "Arcturus"?
ELIOT. Practically none, I gather.
AGNES. Precisely. (*Worried*) After I submitted it, I wondered whether "Saturn" would've been better.
ELIOT. No.
AGNES. Or perhaps "Mercury"?
ELIOT. No.
AGNES. Anyway, that was weeks ago. I should've heard by now.
ELIOT. Cheer up, Aggie. They're saving it for their front cover.
AGNES. Oh, Mr Barlow! Really? (*She picks up the empty carton*) Well, I'm going to post these in the village. (*She moves up* C) I won't be long.
ELIOT (*sitting on the divan*) No hurry. Take your time.

(AGNES *exits* L *in the hall. There is a brief pause.*
DENISE *enters from the garden*)

DENISE (*moving* C) Eliot?
ELIOT. How long have you been out there?
DENISE. Not long. I almost blundered in on you and the Poet Laureate.
ELIOT (*rising and moving to the bar; irritably*) Do you have to sneak in this way? Couldn't you come round the front?
DENISE. I wanted to see you alone. (*Pause*) Not very affectionate, are we? (*She sees the TV set*) What's this? Television in the house of Barlow? Does Paula know?
ELIOT (*turned away*) Not yet.
DENISE. Another surprise? Like her nightgown?
ELIOT (*crossing to* LC; *coldly*) If you must know, it's a present from Guthrie.
DENISE (*turning to him*) I expected a warmer welcome than this.
ELIOT. I've just come back from the hospital. The doctors tell me nothing has changed. Paula may regain her memory eventually, but it isn't very likely just now.
DENISE. Well, if there's the faintest possibility that she can remember . . .
ELIOT. That's not the point. You lied to me yesterday. You told me Paula was faking her amnesia.
DENISE (*contritely*) Darling, I'm sorry. I didn't mean to lie.
ELIOT. You threatened me. You were ready to ruin me if you couldn't have your way. After all I've done—after everything I've given you—you were ready to destroy me.
DENISE (*crossing down* L; *tearfully*) Eliot, I didn't want to lie to you —I didn't want to hurt you—but I couldn't help myself. (*She turns to him*) You know I love you.
ELIOT (*moving to* R *of her*) If you love me, how could you threaten to go to the police?
DENISE. Eliot, I didn't mean it.
ELIOT. How can I trust you now? How can I be sure of you?

Scene 3   PORTRAIT OF MURDER

DENISE (*moving close to him*) Dearest, I'd die if anything came between us.

(ELIOT *is deliberately silent*)

Eliot, please—you must believe me. You're all that matters—nothing else—nor the money . . .

ELIOT (*bluntly*) Of course the money matters. It's gone into your shop—the clothes on your back. You have a champagne appetite, Denise. You've been damned expensive.

DENISE. Darling, you're generous—but you don't deny yourself anything.

ELIOT. And where do you think the money comes from? Those cheques you reminded me of—those securities. Denise, you want us to be together? We've got to have Paula's money. (*He moves to the desk, picks up some letters, crosses to the bar and signs them*)

(DENISE *watches Eliot for a few moments then crosses to the coffee-table and touches the TV set*)

DENISE. Eliot—(*casually*) where are you going to put this thing? (*She sits on the divan*)

ELIOT (*looking up*) What? Oh, that depends on Paula. It's her set.

DENISE. She complains about being bored with her baths, doesn't she? Perhaps if she had TV to look at . . . (*She pauses briefly*) I was reading only last week—"Electrical appliance falls into bath. Tragic accident in Maida Vale". (*She sighs*) Always in Maida Vale.

ELIOT (*leaning over the back of the divan; amused*) Everything's a lethal weapon to you, now, isn't it?

DENISE. Everybody knows Paula is still clumsy and unsure of herself. The police would never question an accidental electrocution.

ELIOT. A second accident? Ten days after she's home from the hospital? No, Denise. Much too risky.

DENISE. Can you suggest a better way?

ELIOT (*patting her head*) I've already thought of one. (*He moves to the fireplace*) Her doctors don't know when Paula will recover her memory—and Jim Guthrie suspects she'll never write again. A woman like Paula—her memory gone—her career ended—(*he turns to the fireplace*) what has she got to live for?

DENISE (*rising; slowly*) Suicide?

ELIOT. Dr Schuyler at the hospital will testify to her fits of depression. Both Schuyler and Kendall prescribed sedatives—tranquillizers . . .

DENISE. An overdose of sleeping pills?

ELIOT. No, no—too obvious. But the baths she takes—the good doctors prescribed them to aid healing and relax her. (*He pauses briefly. Softly*) Just imagine what can happen. Let's suppose she takes a pill or two—with my help. She undresses—gets into her bath. It's quite warm—and so relaxing—much too relaxing. Before she knows it . . . (*He makes a significant, downward gesture with his hand to indicate*

Paula *slipping below the surface of the water; indeed, being helped to drown with his assistance*)

(DENISE *watches Eliot in horrified, admiring fascination. She nods her understanding and assent, as if hypnotized*)

DENISE (*softly*) Yes—yes, I see.
ELIOT (*smoothly*) No risk at all.

(DENISE *looks at* ELIOT *in silence for a moment, then embraces him. The telephone rings. They ignore it*)

PAULA (*off upstairs; calling*) Eliot.

(*The telephone continues to ring*)

ELIOT (*to Denise*) You'd better go. And don't try to call me. I'll ring you from a booth.
DENISE. Come to the flat. Try to get away.
ELIOT. I'll call you.
PAULA (*off upstairs; calling*) Eliot!
ELIOT (*calling*) Yes, Paula. I'll answer it.

(DENISE *holds on to Eliot's arm*)

(*He pushes her away*) Hurry. (*He goes to the telephone and lifts the receiver*)

(DENISE *looks up the stairs then exits into the garden*)

(*Into the telephone*) Hello? . . . Oh, hello, Logan . . . (*He listens irritably*)

(PAULA, *unseen by Eliot, enters down the stairs*)

No—sorry—I can't disturb her just now . . . Yes, in the bath—doctor's orders . . .

(PAULA *moves* C. ELIOT *sees* PAULA *and motions with the receiver, offering to let her talk, but she quickly demurs*)

All right—of course I'll tell her . . . Yes . . . Thanks for calling . . . Good-bye. (*He replaces the receiver*)
PAULA. Tod Logan?
ELIOT. Did you want to talk to him?
PAULA. Oh, no, Eliot.
ELIOT. Well, we can do without Logan. A fair painter but a first-class trouble-maker. Playing practical jokes is Logan's substitute for sex. I break out in spots when the man's near me.
PAULA. They why did I make so much of him?
ELIOT. We're adults, Paula. (*He moves to* L *of her*) We've never chosen one another's friends.
PAULA. Did I have many friends?
ELIOT. Darling, your work is published the world over. You know all kinds of people.
PAULA. But are they my friends?

ELIOT. Paula, like many writers, you weren't particularly fond of any one person.
PAULA. Eliot, I've been thinking about what Agnes said.
ELIOT. Paula, I explained that to you yesterday.
PAULA. I must know the truth about myself. If I knew what happened the day of my accident, I could begin to put all the pieces together.
ELIOT. I can't help you. I've nothing to tell. I left you alone with Agnes that morning and went up to London.
PAULA. Why did you go?
ELIOT. You'd been working yourself to death on your novel and I decided you needed a holiday, so I spent the afternoon with our travel agent in the Strand.
PAULA. Agnes said I was in a foul mood that day. She said I might have overheard you telephoning from my extension upstairs.
ELIOT. There was nothing in my telephone call that could possibly upset you. Besides, you were never one for eavesdropping.
PAULA. But Agnes said . . .
ELIOT. Agnes shouldn't have said anything. I won't have her upsetting you like this.

(PAULA *turns away* R *and sees the TV set*)

PAULA. What's this?
ELIOT. Nothing to do with me. It's a surprise from Jim Guthrie.
PAULA. How sweet of him.
ELIOT (*moving to Paula*) I should've thought of it myself, but you weren't one for the TV in the old days. Appearing on the tube was one thing, looking at it was something else again.
PAULA. I've told you. I've changed. (*She embraces him*) What would Jim Guthrie or George Waller say if they could see me now? Getting sentimental.
ELIOT. I think they'd like it. I know I do.
PAULA. You'd soon tire of me this way. Where shall we put it?
ELIOT. What?
PAULA. The telly, of course. I know. How about upstairs? I get so bored with my silly baths. It would fit perfectly in that little alcove above the bath.
ELIOT. On that shelf? Sorry, darling. Can't be done.
PAULA. Why not? It's the perfect spot for it. I can loll back in my bath and watch the news and plays.
ELIOT. I'm afraid the authorities wouldn't agree. It's too dangerous.
PAULA. Dangerous? Why?
ELIOT. Every television set—even one like this—operates on high voltage. If it fell into your bath or even if you reached up and touched it while you were wet . . .
PAULA. You mean it would be fatal?
ELIOT. Yes, Paula. That's exactly what I mean.

PAULA. I'll be very careful.
ELIOT. Darling, we can't break the law.
PAULA. I'm not asking you to break the law. Just bend it a little. You can run the extension cord from the bedroom.
ELIOT. No, Paula, we can't.
PAULA. But that's silly!
ELIOT. It's for your own protection.
PAULA. Protection? I'm not a child.
ELIOT. Then stop behaving like one.
PAULA. I'm not an imbecile. Why do you treat me like one?
ELIOT. For your own sake, Paula. No.
PAULA (*picking up the TV set*) Well, if you won't do it, I will!
ELIOT (*snatching the set from her*) Sit down! (*He puts the set back on the coffee-table*) I thought you'd changed.
PAULA. I want to change. Why won't you let me?
ELIOT. Paula, don't be hysterical.
PAULA. Why won't you help me? Why won't you do anything I ask?
ELIOT. All right—have it your own way. (*He crosses to the coffee-table, picks up the set and exits upstairs*)
PAULA (*following to the foot of the stairs*) Eliot, don't leave me. Can't you see what it means to be lost in the dark like this? Eliot, I'm sorry, but I've got to know who I am, what I am. I've got to find out what happened to me. Don't hate me, Eliot, help me, help me.

The LIGHTS BLACK-OUT *as—*

the CURTAIN *falls*

ACT II

Scene 1

Scene—*The same. The evening of the same day.*

When the Curtain rises, Guthrie *is standing at the fireplace, documents in hand.* Paula *is at the bar, pouring a drink for Guthrie.*

Paula. Please say "when", Jim. I haven't the faintest idea how you like your drinks.
Guthrie. If you want a rule of thumb—or Guthrie's Basic Principle—don't let the glasss overflow. (*He watches her*) That's fine, Paula. (*He reaches over the divan and takes the glass*) Thank you. Cheers! (*He drinks*)
Paula. Do you drink very much, Jim?
Guthrie. I've done my share. But we won't analyse my reasons for it. (*He puts his glass on the coffee-table*)
Paula (*moving below the divan*) Eliot should be back soon. He said he wouldn't be long.
Guthrie (*indicating his documents*) Well, here are the contracts. When they want something in California, they don't waste any time. Not just air mail—but insured, special handling and signed receipt requested.
Paula (*taking the documents; in mock dismay*) They seem to be heavier than my story. I hope you don't expect me to read all this.
Guthrie. You know, a year ago—even though Eliot handled your business affairs—you checked every comma in every contract with him.
Paula (*putting the documents on the coffee-table*) I'm ten months old now, Jim. (*She sits on the divan*) How many infants do you know who can understand a contract?
Guthrie. Well, it's a thing of beauty. I fought them on every clause. (*He picks up his glass*)
Paula. What do you want me to do about it?
Guthrie. Go over it, first.

(Eliot *enters from the garden*)

(*He sits in the armchair* r) I never let my clients sign something they haven't read.
Paula. I think we'd better wait for Eliot.

(Eliot *moves to* l *of the divan*)

Guthrie. We were just talking about you, Eliot.

ELIOT. Hello, Jim. Been here long?
GUTHRIE (*indicating his drink*) This long.
ELIOT (*crossing to Guthrie*) No time at all. Let me freshen it for you. (*He takes Guthrie's glass, moves to the bar and refills the glass*)
PAULA. Jim's brought the contracts, Eliot.
ELIOT. So I see.
PAULA. He wants us to read them together.

(ELIOT *gives the drink to Guthrie*)

GUTHRIE. Cheers!
ELIOT. Cheers! (*He drinks*) All right—I'll read them. (*To Paula*) It's purely a formality—(*he sits* L *of Paula on the divan*) like the blood rites of the ancient Incas.
GUTHRIE (*grinning*) Only not as painful.

(AGNES *enters down the stairs. She wears her hat and coat and carries an overnight bag*)

Oh, hello, Agnes.
AGNES (*moving* C) Mr Guthrie . . .
GUTHRIE. Taking off somewhere?
AGNES. I'm going to spend a day or two with my brother in Hastings.
PAULA. I told her to visit her family and relax. She's been working much too hard.
AGNES. I do appreciate it—but it isn't urgent, you know. I can go later.
PAULA. Agnes, I insist. Eliot and I can manage by ourselves—can't we, dear?
ELIOT. It'll be a struggle, but we'll try to swing it.
AGNES. We-ell—if you really want me to—I can hardly refuse, can I?
ELIOT. I'll give you a lift in a minute, Agnes.
AGNES. Thank you, Mr Barlow.
PAULA. Sit down, Agnes.

(AGNES *sits on the stool* C)

I've been asking Agnes about the old days, Jim. I'm going to start on you next.

(GUTHRIE *glances at Eliot, then responds warily*)

GUTHRIE. Oh—are you?

(ELIOT *rises and moves above the divan*)

PAULA. I mean to find out all about you—your past history—all the lady novelists who pursue you . . .

SCENE 1 — PORTRAIT OF MURDER

GUTHRIE. Agents seldom arouse female passion. Actors do that—right, Agnes?
AGNES (*blushing*) Oh, I—I really couldn't say.
PAULA (*to Guthrie*) Well, I think you're very attractive. Did I think so in the old days, Eliot?
ELIOT. Why don't you ask Jim?
GUTHRIE. If I were you, Paula, I'd forget the old days and concentrate on the present. Things will come back to you.
PAULA. Jim, I look at myself in the mirror—and it's blank. There's no reflection of the past behind me. (*Painfully*) I've got to know the truth about myself.
ELIOT (*gently*) Darling, we all want to help you. Surely you know that.
GUTHRIE. Of course we do. What do your doctors say?
PAULA. They tell me to be patient.
GUTHRIE. Then I'm in good company.
PAULA. You don't understand—not any of you. You say I'm a writer—but how can I write if I'm empty inside? A writer's raw material is past experience—remembered emotion—all the things I've been robbed of.
GUTHRIE. You remember these last ten months. Write about your life in the hospital.
ELIOT. I've suggested that. So has Dr Schuyler.
PAULA (*despairingly*) I haven't a thought in my head. I don't even have the desire to put anything on paper.
ELIOT. How many times have we heard her say that, Aggie?
AGNES. We-ell—let me see . . .
GUTHRIE. Paula, every writer I've ever known suffers these agonizing black periods. I've known you to sit for days—staring blindly at your typewriter—or trying to dictate five consecutive words to Agnes.
AGNES. That's true. You'd say you couldn't even spell "cat"—and you couldn't.
PAULA (*sighing*) Perhaps you're right. (*She pauses briefly*) It's getting late, Agnes. I don't want you to miss your train.
AGNES. Are you sure you want me to go?
PAULA. Now, stop worrying about me and get out of here.
ELIOT. Let's go, Aggie.

(AGNES *rises*)

(*He collects the documents from the coffee-table*) I'll read these contracts the minute I get back. (*He crosses and puts the documents in the desk drawer*)
GUTHRIE. Take your time.
ELIOT (*moving up* C) C'mon, Aggie.
AGNES (*moving up* C) Good-bye.
PAULA. Good-bye, Agnes.
GUTHRIE (*rising*) Drive carefully.

ELIOT. I'm always careful.

(ELIOT *and* AGNES *exit into the hall. There is a pause as* GUTHRIE *moves to the bar and puts down his glass*)

GUTHRIE (*quietly*) What's wrong, Paula?
PAULA. Eliot and I had a slight row before you came.
GUTHRIE. Nothing serious, I hope?
PAULA. Not really. But I decided if I got Agnes out of the house, Elliot and I could—feel alone.
GUTHRIE (*moving above the divan*) Might be a good idea. It's been a long time since you and Eliot were really alone together.

(PAULA *turns and kneels on the divan*)

PAULA (*slowly*) Jim, you knew me before Eliot ever came into my life. What was I like when you first met me?
GUTHRIE. First of all, *Weep for Adonais* came unsolicited by post. I had no idea what you were like.
PAULA. What did you imagine me to be?
GUTHRIE. Almost anything. (*He sits* L *of Paula on the divan*) A Siamese cat fancier—the spinster daughter of a retired military man. (*Back in the past; softly*) Then you came to my office—pretty but gawky, with your dreams spilling out of you. Completely honest and defenceless. Very much as you are now. But you changed.
PAULA. Is that why you stopped being in love with me?
GUTHRIE. Who told you that?
PAULA. Denise. She said . . .
GUTHRIE (*shortly*) Denise talks too much. (*Gruffly*) You married Eliot. I'm old-fashioned enough not to covet another man's wife. But you've been my best client—so I couldn't keep away.
PAULA. How did you happen to rescue me last November?
GUTHRIE. I loathe that word "rescue". It makes me sound like a St Bernard. (*He is irritated and disturbed by the stirring of old memories*)
PAULA (*softly*) Please tell me about it, Jim.
GUTHRIE. Frankly, Paula, I don't want to.

(*Soft music is heard. The* LIGHTS *start to dim*)

PAULA (*rising*) Do you know what it means to know nothing about oneself? (*She crosses to* LC) It's torture.
GUTHRIE (*giving in*) All right, all right. (*He looks at Paula*) The truth is—I'd been here earlier in the day.
PAULA (*puzzled*) You had? Eliot didn't tell me—and it wasn't in the papers.
GUTHRIE (*rising*) No need to tell them about it.

(*The* LIGHTS BLACK-OUT.
PAULA *exits to the study.*
GUTHRIE *exits into the hall*)

(*Off in the* BLACK-OUT) We'd talked on the phone the night before.

You'd done twenty pages and were ecstatic. But when I phoned the next morning, you snapped my head off and hung up on me. I'd heard from George Waller earlier—so I got in my car and drove down here to see you. Nobody answered the door when I arrived—shortly before noon.

(*The* LIGHTS *come up. The room is empty.*
GUTHRIE *enters from the hall, moves* C *and looks around*)

(*He calls*) Paula? Agnes? Anybody home?
MRS BARLOW (*off in the study; peevishly*) Jim? That you, Jim?
GUTHRIE (*calling*) Yes, Paula. The door was off the latch. I let myself in.
MRS BARLOW (*off*) I'll be with you in a minute.
GUTHRIE (*calling*) No hurry. Take your time. (*He sits on the divan, picks up a newspaper from the coffee-table and glances at it perfunctorily*)

(MRS BARLOW *enters from the study. Her mood is ugly and bitter*)

Oh, hello, Paula. (*He indicates the newspaper*) Who's reading the want-ads? Eliot looking for a job?
MRS BARLOW (*moving to the stairs; icily*) I don't find that amusing, Jim.
GUTHRIE. My apologies to Eliot. (*He puts the newspaper on the coffee-table*)
MRS BARLOW. My God—(*she moves down* LC) my head's splitting right down the middle.
GUTHRIE. Sorry to hear it. Where is everybody?
MRS BARLOW. Gone, naturally. (*She crosses to the fireplace*) I could be dying but no-one gives a damn.
GUTHRIE. Paula, I wouldn't be here if I didn't care about you.
MRS BARLOW (*with her back to him*) I didn't ask you to come.
GUTHRIE. What's troubling you? When I talked to you last night, you couldn't have been happier.
MRS BARLOW. That was last night.
GUTHRIE. Writers! (*Wryly*) You ride an emotional switchback—round and round—up and down. Me, I keep my feet on the ground —so I'm an agent.
MRS BARLOW (*turning and crossing to* LC) Yes. Hopelessly subnormal.
GUTHRIE (*grinning*) Not quite. I'm not a publisher.
MRS BARLOW. I'll admit you're not in George Waller's category.
GUTHRIE (*rising; casually*) George called me this morning. (*He moves to* R *of Mrs Barlow*) He can't wait to read the new novel.
MRS BARLOW. He'll *have* to wait.
GUTHRIE. You told him he'd get it this week.
MRS BARLOW. I don't care what I told him.

(GUTHRIE *moves above the divan*)

If George Waller's father hadn't made a fortune out of canning mackerel and selling it for salmon, George Waller would be cleaning fish instead of publishing books for a living.

GUTHRIE (*mildly*) You've no cause to complain about George.

MRS BARLOW (*facing him*) Who's your client, Mr Guthrie? Me or that squalid little foetus?

GUTHRIE. What's the matter with you?

MRS BARLOW. Is it a crime to be bored? I'm sick to death with George Waller—this house—the novel—everything.

(ELIOT *enters from the garden*)

ELIOT. Oh, hello, Jim. When'd you get here?

GUTHRIE. A few minutes ago. I shan't be staying long.

MRS BARLOW (*to Eliot; coldly*) Agnes said you'd gone up to London.

ELIOT. Not yet. I forgot my wallet. Can't get far without that. (*He pauses briefly*) Agnes leave for Brighton yet?

MRS BARLOW (*curtly*) She's gone.

ELIOT (*after a brief pause*) Am I interrupting anything?

MRS BARLOW. My agent doesn't usually come to see you, does he?

ELIOT (*quietly*) Well, it's one of those days, Jim. Excuse me.

(ELIOT *exits into the hall*)

GUTHRIE (*moving to her*) Bored with Eliot, too, Paula?

MRS BARLOW (*crossing to the fireplace*) I'm bored with everybody and everything.

GUTHRIE. You're always like this when you're on the home stretch. As soon as you write your last page, get Eliot to take you away for a long holiday.

MRS BARLOW. I want to get away now—by myself. My life's a mess, Jim. I've got to sort myself out—decide my future—without interference.

GUTHRIE. What are you saying? You've never been more successful. You're at the height of your career...

MRS BARLOW. Successful! What has it all brought me?

GUTHRIE. Have you discussed this with Eliot?

MRS BARLOW. Eliot has nothing to do with my writing. He's my husband—not my collaborator. He doesn't write my books—he only lives off them. (*She moves below the divan. Flatly*) Now tell George Waller I want a thousand pounds.

GUTHRIE. A cool thousand? When you're running out on him?

MRS BARLOW. I'm not asking for charity. It all comes out of my royalties.

GUTHRIE. Why make things unpleasant between you? If you insist on going away now, pay for your own trip.

MRS BARLOW (*crossing to* LC) I'm not dipping into my capital, Jim. Earn your commission for a change. I want that thousand by noon tomorrow.

GUTHRIE (*facing her; helplessly*) Paula, I swear you baffle me.

Yesterday you were busy and happy—in love with your husband . . .

MRS BARLOW. Oh, God—you and Little Nell!

(ELIOT *enters from the hall*)

ELIOT. Well, I'll be getting along. Next time you have an hour to spare, Jim, I'd like to discuss publicity for Paula's new book.

GUTHRIE. Give me a ring, Eliot. We'll all have lunch.

ELIOT. How about next week? Paula ought to be finished by then.

MRS BARLOW (*viciously*) For God's sake, I'm sick to death of the novel. If you're going to London, go.

ELIOT. I'm going, Paula. Did you take your migraine pills?

MRS BARLOW. Damn the migraine pills! Just leave me alone.

ELIOT. All right, dear. See you this evening. (*He moves to the garden door*)

MRS BARLOW. If I'm here.

(ELIOT, *alarmed, stiffens and moves* C)

ELIOT. What . . . ?

MRS BARLOW. The way I feel, I may want to get away from the house.

ELIOT. If your migraine's kicking up, you'd better stay close to home.

GUTHRIE. He's right, Paula.

MRS BARLOW. Why don't you both chain me to my typewriter while you're at it?

ELIOT. Darling—look—I'll cancel my thing in London and stay home with you.

MRS BARLOW. God, no! You know I won't stir from the house all day.

ELIOT (*relieved*) That's better, dear. Going back to London, Jim?

GUTHRIE. As soon as your wife chucks me out.

(ELIOT *exits into the hall.* GUTHRIE *moves to the bar and pours a drink for himself*)

(*After a pause*) You were pretty rough on him, weren't you?

MRS BARLOW. Is marriage counselling part of your service, now? Or do you charge extra for that?

GUTHRIE. No charge. (*Resignedly*) You *do* need a change of scene. Take the week-end off, why don't you? Then come back and finish the book. After that, you can splurge on a real holiday and enjoy it.

MRS BARLOW. How much does George Waller pay you to take his side against me?

GUTHRIE (*with a step towards her*) If you must know, George told me this morning. "No book, no advance."

MRS BARLOW. Oh, did he? (*Viciously*) Then tell that little guttersnipe he'll never get this book. He'll never publish another word I write.

GUTHRIE (*moving to the bar*) For God's sake, Paula . . .
MRS BARLOW. That insignificant little miser. (*She moves to the bar*) He isn't the only publisher in London. (*She snatches up the telephone receiver*) I know a dozen other houses that would give anything to sign me up.
GUTHRIE (*grabbing the receiver*) Don't be idiotic!
MRS BARLOW (*struggling for the receiver*) Give it to me.
GUTHRIE. Behave yourself. You've got an air-tight contract with George Waller. No other house will touch your stuff.
MRS BARLOW. You saw to that, didn't you? Well, I don't need you—and I don't need George Waller. I'll break my contract.
GUTHRIE. Paula—don't be childish! (*He replaces the receiver*)
MRS BARLOW (*exploding*) Childish? (*She moves to the fireplace*) You think my books come to me through spirit-writing? I rip them out of me—I agonize over every word.

(*Soft music is heard*)

Then blood-suckers like you and George Waller tell me—"Don't be childish!" (*Wildly*) Now, get out—leave me alone! I don't care what you do—but get out—we're finished!

(*The* LIGHTS *start to dim.*
GUTHRIE *exits into the hall. There is a crash of music and the* LIGHTS BLACK-OUT. *The music continues.*
MRS BARLOW *exits in the* BLACK-OUT.
GUTHRIE *and* PAULA *enter in the* BLACK-OUT *and take up their previous positions,* PAULA *seated* C *of the divan and* GUTHRIE *seated* L *of her. The* LIGHTS *come up. The music fades*)

PAULA (*sick with self-loathing*) I feel so ashamed—so ashamed.
GUTHRIE. I warned you, Paula. Few of us can look back and be content with what we were. (*He rises, moves to the bar and refills his glass*) I'm sorry. I should've kept my mouth shut.
PAULA. How could you bear to see me again in that day? Why did you come back?
GUTHRIE. You called my office—told my secretary you had to see me again—something about a lawyer. (*He resumes his seat on the divan*) My girl reached me at George Waller's. I drove straight here with his cheque.
PAULA. You got my advance?
GUTHRIE. I was mercenary. I wanted you to finish your book.
PAULA. Why did I ask about a lawyer?
GUTHRIE. That's your secret, Paula. It's buried with everything else you can't remember. Gone with the manuscript that burned up.
PAULA (*soberly*) Perhaps I have another secret. The way I behaved that day—perhaps it wasn't an accident at all. It's possible I tried to kill myself.

GUTHRIE. Paula, you were too strong-willed—to be blunt about it, too selfish—to attempt suicide.

(PAULA *rises, turns slowly to the fireplace and looks up at the portrait.* GUTHRIE *watches her*)

PAULA. I hate what I was.
GUTHRIE. Now you're like the rest of us. You can feel guilty about the past.
PAULA. Agnes says Eliot's always been devoted to me. But now I don't know if I even loved him.
GUTHRIE. You did—in your own way. Eliot was something you wanted, Paula, so you married him. You were possessive and demanding—and you often treated him abominably. But I never doubted your love for him.
PAULA (*with a step towards him*) Did he love me?
GUTHRIE. Eliot's shrewd and canny. He's always looked out for your interests.
PAULA (*defensively*) I know he's loyal. He's been devoted to me since my accident. I know that much.
GUTHRIE. You're a wealthy woman, Paula—and your royalties keep rolling in.
PAULA. You don't like Eliot, do you?
GUTHRIE. I told you I'm old-fashioned. I think husbands should support their wives. Unfortunately, you earn more than enough for both of you.
PAULA (*sitting* R *of Guthrie on the divan*) Is that what changed me? Success?
GUTHRIE. It makes terrible demands on people. The pressures can be tremendous.
PAULA. But how could you bear to put up with me?
GUTHRIE. Every so often I'd catch a glimpse of the girl who walked into my office and said, "You really like my novel?" (*He holds her hand. Softly*) Now she's back again.
PAULA. Jim—the girl I was can never come back. After what I've found out about myself, how can I ever be like her again?

(TOD *enters from the hall, carrying a bouquet of red roses. He stops short in exaggerated surprise*)

TOD. Hello? Story conference?
GUTHRIE (*coldly*) Hello, Logan.
TOD. Guthrie. (*He crosses to Paula*) Paula, dear. I've decided carnations aren't your flower, now. (*He presents the bouquet*) Red roses, my sweet.
PAULA. Thank you, Tod.
TOD. Let me put them in water for you. (*He moves up* C *with the bouquet*) Where is everyone? I haven't seen your loving helpmate or faithful secretary in aeons. I miss them—as I'm sure they miss me.

PAULA. Agnes took off for Hastings for a few days. Eliot drove her to the station.
TOD (*moving above the divan*) So we're alone at last—so to speak. The flowers.

(TOD *exits into the hall*)

GUTHRIE (*rising and moving to the bar*) I gather I'm the party of the third part. (*He puts his glass on the bar*) I'll leave you two alone.
PAULA. You're not leaving, Jim? What about the contracts?
GUTHRIE. Have Eliot go over them. I'll send a messenger for them tomorrow.
PAULA. Must you run?
GUTHRIE. I'm a Philistine. I always get uncomfortable around artists.
PAULA. Including me?
GUTHRIE. You're an exception—now. (*He glances at his watch*) I have to run, anyway. I want to phone the office before my secretary calls it a day.
PAULA. You can do it from here, Jim.
GUTHRIE. I'll do it on the road—when I stop for petrol.
PAULA. Well, thank you for everything—especially for the TV set. It was very thoughtful of you.

(TOD *enters from the hall with the roses in a vase, which he puts on the desk*)

TOD. From my own garden, I'll have you know. Pollinated with my own lily-white hands.
GUTHRIE. Good-bye, Paula. (*He moves up* C) I'll call tomorrow.
TOD (*moving* C) Leaving already, Guthrie?
GUTHRIE. I'm allergic—to roses.

(GUTHRIE *exits into the hall*
PAULA *rises, moves to the left end of the divan and sits*)

TOD. Isn't it marvellous? The classic bourgeois hatred for the artist. Agnes has the same contempt for me.
PAULA. How can you say that, Tod? Agnes is completely honest and straightforward.
TOD. You didn't feel that way about her in the old days. You once said she was such a bird brain, it's a pity she couldn't take off.
PAULA. Then why did I keep her on?
TOD (*crossing to the fireplace*) You said it was easier to put up with her poetry than break in a new secretary with other liabilities. (*He looks up at the portrait then studies Paula*)

(PAULA *is disturbed by his scrutiny*)

You know, I'll have to paint you again, dear. When shall we start?
PAULA. I—I'll have to ask Eliot.
TOD. Judas, you *have* changed! When I suggested doing your

SCENE 1   PORTRAIT OF MURDER

portrait the first time, you simply said, "How much will it cost me?" Which was fair enough. Your money paid for it, not Eliot's.

PAULA. I'm beginning to understand why Eliot doesn't like you, Tod.

TOD (*moving* C) You think that's why he's kept me from seeing you? Or could there be another reason?

PAULA (*puzzled*) Another reason?

TOD. Think about it. This is the first time we've been alone since you came home from the hospital.

PAULA. But today's the first time you've even phoned me.

TOD. So Eliot told you about *that* call.

PAULA. You mean you've called before?

TOD. Almost every day. Actually, it started before you came home. I tried to see you in the hospital—but Eliot . . .

PAULA. That was my fault, Tod. I was afraid to see anyone.

TOD. I can understand that. If my house had blown up in my face, I'd scream if anyone asked me for a match. But do you think it's wise to cut yourself off from everyone? Do you think it's safe. (*He pauses briefly*) Frankly, darling, I can't sleep at night, worrying about you.

PAULA. Tod, is this one of your silly jokes?

TOD. Darling, I play tricks on dolts and peasants—never on you.

(*Soft music is heard*)

But ever since this accident of yours—if it was an accident . . .

PAULA. Of course it was. (*Anxiously*) Wasn't it?

(*The* LIGHTS *start to dim*)

TOD. So everyone insists. The truth is, Paula, the day of the fire —just three hours before that gas boiler exploded—I dropped by to see you—around two-thirty that afternoon.

(*The* LIGHTS BLACK-OUT.

TOD *and* PAULA *exit in the* BLACK-OUT)

(*Off*) You'd hung your portrait just the week before. I still delighted in looking at it—as I do with any work of art. I came in through the garden, as usual.

(*The music continues as the* LIGHTS *come up. The room is empty.*

TOD *enters from the garden, moves to the fireplace and studies the portrait.*

MRS BARLOW *enters down the stairs. Seen through* TOD'S *eyes she is genuinely troubled, a harried and unhappy woman rather than the possessive neurotic of the earlier scenes. The music fades*)

(*He turns*) Paula, my sweet.

(MRS BARLOW *moves down* L)

(*He indicates the portrait with a flourish*) You know, Angel, you should've been a duchess, like Goya's maja. And I should've painted two versions of you, like Goya—this one and a nude—"Paula Stepping from her Bath". I can see those rosy flesh tones—the iridescent pearls of water caressing your bare—shoulders.

Mrs Barlow (*crossing to the fireplace*) Oh, stop chattering, Tod. You make me nervous.

Tod (*crossing to* c) A thousand pardons—memsahib. (*Conspiratorially*) Are we alone?

Mrs Barlow. Eliot's in London.

Tod (*moving up* c) And the fair Agnes?

Mrs Barlow. Gone to Brighton.

Tod (*moving down* l) You take Aggie too much for granted, angel. How do you know Eliot hasn't gone to Brighton instead of London?

Mrs Barlow (*moving* c) There are times when you're amusing, Tod, but this isn't one of them.

Tod. You misjudge my role, Mrs Barlow. I fancy myself as a court painter, not a court jester.

(Mrs Barlow *paces to the fireplace*)

If you'll sit somewhere, my love, we might establish communication.

Mrs Barlow. Why did you have to drop in? Can't you see I'm in a state?

Tod. Hit a snag with the book?

Mrs Barlow. I'm not worried about that.

Tod. Then what? Is George Waller trying to act like a publisher again?

(Mrs Barlow *ignores his query, paces nervously, then moves* c *and confronts him*)

Mrs Barlow. Tod—I wouldn't dare say this to anyone else. But you understand me.

Tod. Of course. We're identical twins.

(Mrs Barlow *moves to Tod*)

(*Still amused*) Paula, why so dramatic? Has Eliot threatened to go back on the boards?

Mrs Barlow (*crossing to the fireplace*) It isn't Eliot.

Tod. Well, in that case—the natural assumption is . . .

(*The front-door bell rings*)

(*Blandly*) Shall I see who it is, dear?

Mrs Barlow (*sharply*) Never mind. You can go now.

Tod. The old heave-ho?

Mrs Barlow (*curtly*) I want to be alone, Tod.

(Tod *moves towards the front door*)

Not that way. Through the garden.

(TOD *halts and eyes her quizzically, then exits to the garden.*
MRS BARLOW *goes to the garden door to peer after him and then, satisfied he has gone, she exits into the hall*)

(*Off*) Oh—it's you.

(*The telephone rings*)

DENISE (*off*) I came as soon as I could—darling.

(DENISE *enters from the hall and moves down* LC.
MRS BARLOW *follows her on, goes to the telephone and lifts the receiver*)

Why so anxious to see me, Paula?
MRS BARLOW (*into the telephone*) Hello? . . . Yes, speaking . . . You can? . . . Yes, I'll be here . . . Certainly . . . Good-bye. (*She replaces the receiver and turns to Denise*) What did Eliot say when I called you at the shop?
DENISE. Eliot . . . ? Paula, dear—if you're joking—and if Agnes is listening . . .
MRS BARLOW. Agnes isn't here. I know Eliot was with you.
DENISE. Aren't you letting your migraine upset you?
MRS BARLOW (*moving to Denise*) It isn't migraine that's bothering me.
DENISE (*moving up* RC) It never is, is it? Your headaches are just an excuse to make everyone miserable.
MRS BARLOW. Drunks and friends always tell the truth, don't they?
DENISE. If it weren't for your trashy best-sellers, no-one would tolerate you.
MRS BARLOW. You two-faced little hypocrite!
DENISE. Least of all your husband.
MRS BARLOW. Eliot is my property, Denise. Keep your hands off.
DENISE. It's the other way round, Paula.
MRS BARLOW. Stay away from him, Denise.
DENISE. You paid him to marry you—and it's more than his acting ever brought him.
MRS BARLOW. And what do you think you can bring him?
DENISE. Everything you don't give him. When did you find out?
MRS BARLOW (*moving above the divan*) I heard him phone you this morning. I listened on my bedroom extension.
DENISE. He did get careless, didn't he?
MRS BARLOW. Oh, I know about his one-night romances—his cheap café pick-ups—(*bitterly*) but never in my own house.
DENISE. I knew you'd found out this morning, when Eliot told me how you humiliated him in front of Jim Guthrie.
MRS BARLOW. So you were together.

DENISE. Oh, yes—all cosy and snug—until he left for London. He ordered me not to see you, but after he'd gone I decided to give you one last chance to settle everything sensibly. (*She pauses briefly*) Eliot wants to marry me, Paula.

MRS BARLOW (*contemptuously*) I don't see you taking on a husband who can't support himself.

DENISE. You can afford to make a settlement on him.

MRS BARLOW (*turning to her*) Pay him for a divorce I'll never give him? I had no idea you had a weakness for fantasy.

DENISE. You wouldn't have the money you do if it weren't for the publicity Eliot's got you—the investments he's made for you.

MRS BARLOW (*moving to her*) So that's what he's told you? Well, you can tell him this. Unless he stops this cheap, leprous little affair —and drops you immediately . . .

DENISE. He'll never do that.

MRS BARLOW. You don't know my husband. When he has to make a choice—between you and everything I can give him . . .

DENISE (*smugly*) Paula, he's already made his choice—or, shall we say, made his bed?

MRS BARLOW. Get out! Get out of my house!

DENISE. You're being very foolish, Paula. You're making a fatal mistake. I'll give you one more chance.

MRS BARLOW. Don't try to bargain with me. Get out of here— get out.

(DENISE *gives Mrs Barlow a look, then exits into the hall*)

(*She runs up* c *and screams after Denise*) Don't dare come inside my house again. You hear me? Don't ever come back.

(MRS BARLOW *exits into the hall.*
TOD *enters nonchalantly from the garden, and moves above the divan.*
MRS BARLOW *enters slowly from the hall; then sees Tod*)

How typical of you, Tod.

TOD. For your own benefit, angel. (*Gloating*) I've warned you against that poisonous little wench. You can't say I haven't.

MRS BARLOW. She's young, she's pretty—but she doesn't really mean anything to Eliot. (*Self-persuasive*) Oh, I know he's lazy, selfish, deceitful, a charming liar—I've always known that. But I need him—(*she moves below the divan*) and he needs me. If it weren't for Denise . . .

TOD (*leaning over the back of the divan*) It would be someone else.

MRS BARLOW. Don't say that. (*She sits on the divan. Pleadingly*) Help me, Tod. Tell me what to do.

TOD (*moving* C) Don't you pay Jim Guthrie to handle your unpleasant chores?

MRS BARLOW. I can't go to Jim about this.

TOD. Then set a private detective on Denise.

MRS BARLOW (*dubiously*) What?

TOD. He could provide evidence that will pull her venomous white fangs.
MRS BARLOW. Evidence? What kind?
TOD. All sorts of evidence. (*He crosses to the fireplace*) That's for you to decide, angel. Anything can be arranged—for a price. Then you confront her with it. "Now clear out, you treacherous little bitch, or suffer the consequences."
MRS BARLOW (*rising*) No—I couldn't.

(TOD *crosses to* C)

It might backfire. (*She moves to the fireplace*) I'll have to think of something else.
TOD. Don't think too long, my sweet. Little Denise isn't one to wait for what she wants.

(*Soft music is heard*)

MRS BARLOW. And I'm not one to let the likes of Denise take anything from me. (*She looks at him*) Don't feel too sorry for me, Tod.

(*The* LIGHTS *start to dim*)

I'll get back at her somehow.

(*The* LIGHTS BLACK-OUT. *The music continues.*
MRS BARLOW *exits in the* BLACK-OUT.
PAULA *enters in the* BLACK-OUT. *She and* TOD *take up their previous positions,* PAULA *seated on the right end of the divan and* TOD *seated* R *of her. The* LIGHTS *come up and the music fades*)

TOD. Well, now you know, Paula. I've never spoken to anyone else about it. I didn't want to make trouble. But I had to come and tell you.
PAULA. Not make trouble? Tod, you delight in making mischief.
TOD. Don't you believe me?
PAULA (*rising and moving to* LC; *with her back to him*) Eliot loves me—he's devoted to me. And Denise is my best friend.
TOD (*moving below her then turning to her*) Angel, I quote from your own collected works. "Best friends make the best co-respondents." (*He takes an envelope from his pocket*) Here. Read this. (*He hands the envelope to Paula*)
PAULA (*glancing at the address*) It's addressed to you.
TOD. It came just now—from Dover. Read it.

(PAULA *looks wonderingly at* TOD, *then takes a folded typed sheet from the envelope and slowly reads it aloud*)

PAULA (*reading*) "Dear Mr Logan. Tell Paula Barlow to watch Denise Murray. Next time she might not be lucky. Irene Morgan." (*She looks up*) Irene Morgan? Who is she?
TOD. I don't know. And I'm sure you never knew her.
PAULA. Who can she be? Why should she write to you?

D

TOD. I only know this came in the post this afternoon.
PAULA. I still don't understand. (*She reads slowly*) "Next time she might not be lucky . . ."
TOD. It's hardly ambiguous, you know.
PAULA. You mean—Denise . . . ? (*Shocked*) Tod, no. It was an accident.
TOD. You still think so?
PAULA (*gropingly*) Irene Morgan—somehow it sounds familiar—but who can she be? What does she know? And *how* can she know?
TOD. I'm not a clairvoyant, Paula. Maybe you'd better ask Eliot.
PAULA. No—no, I can't. (*She backs away. Plaintively*) Why would Eliot know anything? Besides, I've only your word to go on.
TOD. You took my word as gospel in the old days.
PAULA (*returning the letter and envelope to Tod*) I don't want to talk about it. (*She moves to the study door*)
TOD (*moving quickly to stop her going*) Paula, I'm your friend.
PAULA. Please go—please.
TOD. All right, I'll go. But there's one more thing, Paula. Remember the day you came home? I asked Denise about an auction in Canterbury.
PAULA. You said someone had told you . . .
TOD. No-one told me. I saw her in Canterbury—with Eliot.
PAULA. Together?
TOD. I can give you the name of the hotel—and the other places they've stayed overnight.

(PAULA *stands speechless with shock*)

Call it snooping, if you like. But I wouldn't spy for everybody, Paula. (*He takes a second letter from his pocket*) Here. This letter's for you.

(TOD *hands the envelope to Paula, then exits into the hall. Left alone,* PAULA *looks at the letter in her hand, afraid to open it. The telephone rings.* PAULA *starts nervously and stands rigid, unable to answer it. It continues to ring. At last she forces herself to go to the telephone and lift the receiver*)

PAULA (*into the telephone*) Hello? . . . (*Apprehensively*) Hello? . . . Who is this? . . . (*Shakily*) I know someone's there. Why don't you say something? . . . (*Sharply*) Hello, hello . . . (*She replaces the receiver, trembling and half afraid to move*)

(ELIOT *enters quietly from the hall, unnoticed by* PAULA)

ELIOT. Well, I saw Agnes off safely.

(PAULA *wheels with a startled gasp*)

Sorry, darling. Didn't mean to make you jump.
PAULA. I—I just answered the phone. It—it frightened me.

ELIOT. Why? What happened?
PAULA (*backing to the study door*) Whoever it was didn't say a word. The receiver simply went dead.
ELIOT (*moving to her*) Well, don't let it upset you. A wrong number, most likely.
PAULA. Yes—yes, I suppose so.
ELIOT (*indicating the letter*) What's that? Mail? Aren't you going to read it?
PAULA (*holding out the letter*) You read it, Eliot.

(ELIOT, *puzzled, takes the letter and reads the address*)

ELIOT. Postmarked Dover. (*He opens the envelope, unfolds the letter inside and reads it in silence*)
PAULA. It's from Irene Morgan, isn't it?
ELIOT (*sharply; surprised*) How do you know that?
PAULA. Read it to me.
ELIOT (*reading*) "Dear Mrs Barlow. Want to stay alive? Then don't get careless around Denise Murray." (*He looks up*) It's signed —"Irene Morgan."
PAULA (*in a whisper*) Yes—I thought so.
ELIOT. How could you? What do you know about Irene Morgan?
PAULA (*groping*) I—I don't know. (*She moves to* L *of the coffee-table*) I think I've heard the name before—but I can't remember where. Do you know her, Eliot?
ELIOT. Of course not. (*He moves down* C) Never heard of her. (*Sharply*) How do you know about her? Try to remember.
PAULA. I—I . . . (*Helplessly*) It's no use. I'm all mixed up now.
ELIOT. How did you know this letter came from her?
PAULA. Tod Logan got one just like this.
ELIOT. Logan? Is that liar gossiping again?
PAULA. It isn't gossip. I saw the note.
ELIOT. ·When? Just now? What did it say? (*Sharply*) Answer me. I've got to know.
PAULA (*after a brief pause*) Eliot—you lied to me. You're in love with Denise. (*Anguished*) Did you know she tried to kill me?

ELIOT, *taken by surprise, cannot answer.*

The LIGHTS BLACK-OUT

SCENE 2

SCENE—*The same. Later the same night.*

When the LIGHTS *come up*, DENISE *is standing by the open study door, letter in hand, talking to* ELIOT, *who is in the study.* DENISE, *tense with fear and hostility, can be triggered into panic by the slightest word or incident.*

DENISE. Eliot—will you please stop rummaging in those files and listen to me? I want to know what we're going to do.

(*There is no answer*)

Eliot! (*Unanswered, she turns from the study door in frustration, goes to the stairs, looks up them, then returns to the study door*) Have you finished?

(ELIOT *enters from the study, a sheaf of letters in his hand, controlling himself with a conscious effort. He is infuriated by the unforeseen developments which now threaten his scheme to do away with his wife. He brushes past Denise without a word, crosses to the divan, sits, sets out the letters on the coffee-table and examines them*)

(*She moves* C) Will you please tell me how some woman in Dover can know about us? And why should her name sound familiar to Paula? I've never heard of Irene Morgan—and you say you never . . .

ELIOT. For God's sake, Denise! I told you to stay away when you called me. Now, stop babbling and let me read.

DENISE (*moving to* L *of the divan*) Stay away? When I get a letter like this? When I'm accused of trying to kill Paula? (*She reads from the letter*) "When she remembers what happened, you'll be blamed, you know—not her husband." (*She looks up*) Who can she be? And what does she mean—I'll be blamed?

(ELIOT *is silent*)

Eliot—I'm talking to you.

ELIOT. Be quiet. Let me finish. (*He reads for a few moments, then looks up*) I thought so. It's all here.

DENISE. What?

ELIOT. Before Paula ran upstairs and locked herself in her room, she remembered where she'd heard of Irene Morgan.

DENISE. Why didn't you tell me?

ELIOT (*putting the letters in his pocket*) I wanted to check first. Agnes told her last week. It's all here in the correspondence files. Irene Morgan first wrote from Dover last December, and she's been writing ever since.

DENISE. Who is she? What does she say?

ELIOT (*rising and moving to the fireplace*) Nothing enlightening. A typical Paula Winsten fan—idolizes her—knows *Weep for Adonais* line by line.

DENISE (*moving below the divan*) Then we still don't know how she could know about us.

ELIOT. No, we don't. But I have her address in Dover, now. I'll drive down there later.

DENISE. Do you think you should?

ELIOT. Denise, I've no other choice. She knows everything that passed between you two that day. (*Angrily*) I told you not to come here. Logan was outside taking in every word. (*He crosses to* LC)

DENISE. I couldn't know that Tod would be here. Eliot, what would happen if Paula went to the police now?
ELIOT. I won't let her go. I won't let her leave the house or use the phone. And I'll make sure she sleeps tonight.
DENISE. The sleeping pills? Tonight?
ELIOT. I can't put it off now.
DENISE (*moving to him*) No, Eliot, we can't. Please, let's drop it. We'll go away somewhere, anywhere. Let's go now while it's safe.
ELIOT. I can't drop it.
DENISE. But if anything happens to Paula a second time?
ELIOT. It's got to be done tonight. Will you get that through your head?
DENISE. No, we can't. There must be some other way. Tell her Tod wrote those letters as a joke, to stir up trouble. You can make her believe that.
ELIOT. It's too late, Denise. (*He closes the study door*)

(PAULA *enters down the stairs, moving stealthily and fearfully, intent on slipping away from the house. She reaches the bottom tread, still unnoticed, then* ELIOT *turns and sees her*)

Paula, darling!

(PAULA *freezes*)

(*He moves towards her*) Denise is here. I asked her to come and talk things out with you.

(PAULA *comes slowly and reluctantly forward*)

DENISE (*moving to* R *of Paula*) Hello, Paula. I—I don't really know what to say. I mean—those letters to you and Tod. I've received one just like it. You mustn't believe them, Paula. They're nothing but lies.
PAULA. Are they?
DENISE. Of course. You tell her, Eliot.
ELIOT. I've already tried to tell her.
PAULA. I've been thinking upstairs. "A fatal mistake," you said the day of the accident.
DENISE. Did I?
PAULA. You know you did. Tod heard you. (*Slowly*) "I'll give you one more chance," you said. "One last chance." (*Deliberately*) It wasn't an accident at all, was it? If Jim Guthrie hadn't ruined your scheme—if I'd died—Eliot would never have learned the truth about you.
DENISE. Eliot? What truth?
PAULA. You tried to kill me.
ELIOT (*crossing down* L *of the divan*) It couldn't be. I'm sure Denise can explain.
DENISE (*bitterly*) Irene Morgan was right, wasn't she? She said I'd be blamed for everything—not you.

PAULA. Eliot . . . ?
DENISE. Of course. I wouldn't know how to make a gas boiler explode.
ELIOT. Stop it, Denise.
PAULA. You mean—all the time—both you and Eliot . . . ?
DENISE. You brought it on yourself, Paula. You're a mean, selfish, cold-hearted bitch. It wouldn't have been murder—no—a public service.
ELIOT. Stop it, Denise, stop it.

(PAULA *faces Eliot in horror. Her world is shattered. Nothing is what she believed it was*)

PAULA (*anguished*) All the time I was in the hospital—all those agonizing months—you were all I had. You gave me the will to live. I trusted you. Why did you do this to me? I thought you loved me! Why didn't you let me die? (*She turns to go*)
ELIOT (*intercepting Paula*) Listen to me.
PAULA (*backing up* LC) Don't touch me.
ELIOT (*seizing her*) Paula, you can't leave. You've got to listen to me.

(DENISE *moves up to the hall entrance*)

PAULA. No—let me go.
ELIOT (*soothingly*) Darling, please. If you'll let me tell you the truth—these letters from Dover . . .
PAULA (*struggling to get away*) Why didn't you let me die? (*She sobs*) I thought you loved me.
ELIOT. Darling, I did—I do—I can explain everything.
PAULA. No. Nothing but lies. All lies. (*She frees herself and dashes towards the front door*)

(DENISE *intercepts* PAULA, *who wheels towards Eliot*)

Let me go, let me go.
ELIOT (*taking her by the arms*) Paula, for God's sake—listen to me. I don't want to hurt you—just let me explain.
PAULA (*wildly*) If you want my money, take it. I'll sign over everything to you—anything you say . . .
ELIOT. Paula, stop it. Stop it. (*He wheels her round towards the divan*)
PAULA. You can have everything. (*She starts hitting him*) Let me go, let me go.

(ELIOT *hits* PAULA. *As she falls behind the divan they knock over the lamp by the divan. The room goes dark; only the door to the garden is highlighted.* ELIOT *kneels beside Paula. There is a long pause, filled with the laboured breathing of* ELIOT *and* DENISE. *The room is dappled with shadow.* DENISE *waits fearfully; then* ELIOT *slowly rises to face her*)

ELIOT. She's dead.
DENISE. Dead! (*She moves up* LC)

ELIOT (*crossing slowly to Denise*) If you'd kept your mouth shut . . .
DENISE. It isn't my fault. (*Sick with fear*) We'll have to face the police now.
ELIOT. Yes.
DENISE (*desperately*) Can't we make it look like an accident? Can't we say she went walking—got lost in the dark—fell in the river . . .
ELIOT. How do we get her there?
DENISE. In your car.
ELIOT. And if someone sees us?
DENISE. Something else, then. We'll take her outside to the road. A hit-and-run accident . . .
ELIOT. And when the police examine my car . . . (*Firmly*) No, Denise. It won't work.
DENISE. Your suicide plan?
ELIOT. No. Your plan.
DENISE. Mine?
ELIOT. Have you forgotten? A fatal accident—in her bath.
DENISE. Her TV set?
ELIOT. It fell into the water. I heard her scream—I ran upstairs to help her but it was too late. (*He pauses briefly*) You lock up down here. I'll go and arrange everything upstairs.

(ELIOT *exits slowly up the stairs.*
DENISE *exits into the hall. The darkened shadow-laced room remains hushed. Only the garden door is still highlighted.*
MRS BARLOW *enters from the garden, high-lighted. She is perfectly poised. She wears a travelling suit and carries a suitcase. She puts the case in the hall. She glances up the stairs, crosses to the phone. Then she notices the new swivel chair and touches it. Still thoughtful, she moves to the staircase and peers upward, then moves to the study door. As she does so, a shadow begins to rise waveringly on the wall behind the divan. A hand appears on the back of the divan, then* PAULA *slowly pulls herself upright. A shadowy figure, dazed and weak, she sways helplessly as she looks around, trying to get her bearings.* MRS BARLOW *turns and sees Paula and crosses to her*)

PAULA (*dazed and inarticulate*) No, no . . . (*She backs away in fear and shock*)
MRS BARLOW. What's wrong? What happened?
PAULA (*incoherently*) Let me go.
MRS BARLOW (*taking Paula by the arm*) You'd better lie down. (*They cross to the study door*) Come in here. Careful—slowly now.

(MRS BARLOW *and* PAULA *exit to the study*)

(*Off*) That's it—here's a cushion. Don't move. I'll call a doctor.
PAULA (*off; faintly*) No—I—I . . .
MRS BARLOW (*off*) Where's Eliot?
PAULA (*off*) Don't know—don't know . . .

(MRS BARLOW *enters from the study. Unruffled, she crosses to the phone*)

ELIOT (*off upstairs*) Denise?

(MRS BARLOW *quickly but calmly moves to the desk chair and seats herself. Its high back is towards the staircase.*
ELIOT, *oblivious to Mrs Barlow's presence, enters down the stairs*)

(*He calls*) Denise, have you finished out there?

(DENISE *enters from the hall*)

(*He turns to face Denise in the shadowed room*) Darling, trust me. Everything will work out all right.

(DENISE *is silent*)

It's what we wanted, isn't it?

DENISE. You've forgotten Irene Morgan.

ELIOT. I haven't forgotten. I'm driving to Dover as soon as we've finished here. (*He switches on the wall-bracket up* R *and the desk lamp, by the switch up* R, *then moves above the divan and freezes with shock when he sees Paula has gone*)

(DENISE *looks behind the divan*)

DENISE. You said she was dead.

ELIOT (*impatiently*) I didn't want another argument with you.

DENISE. You knew she was alive. You lied to me.

ELIOT. Where is she, Denise? We've got to find her.

DENISE. You lied. I won't go through with it—I won't. She's got away—she's gone to the police. I'll tell them everything I know —all about you—everything.

(ELIOT *pulls* DENISE *by her hair. She cries out*)

MRS BARLOW. Eliot, how charming. You've become a violent man.

(*As* ELIOT *and* DENISE *wheel in shock, the swivel chair turns to face them, revealing* MRS BARLOW. *She is in complete charge, savouring every moment.* ELIOT *moves up* L *of the divan*)

Yes, I'm back.

DENISE (*incoherently*) You . . .

MRS BARLOW. Yes, I'm Paula Barlow, Denise.

ELIOT (*slowly*) My wife.

MRS BARLOW. You see, Denise? My husband doesn't question my identity.

DENISE. Then the other one—who is she? What have you done with her?

MRS BARLOW. I've taken her into the study.

(ELIOT *crosses and exits to the study*)

You were much more relaxed in the old days, Denise. (*Musingly*) How did I inscribe my last book to you? "In truest gratitude—for truest friendship."

(ELIOT *enters from the study*)

ELIOT. Who is she, Paula?
MRS BARLOW. What have you done to her, Eliot? She sounded very alarmed when I phoned the house earlier.
ELIOT. Who is she, Paula?
MRS BARLOW. Her name's Irene Morgan.
DENISE. But Irene Morgan wrote those letters.
ELIOT. No. (*He crosses below the divan*) My wife wrote those letters.
MRS BARLOW. Quick as ever, aren't you, dear? (*She rises and crosses to Denise*) Denise, you remember that phone call on that fatal afternoon? That was Irene Morgan. I'd phoned her earlier about her Situation Wanted Ad. I engaged her as my secretary.
DENISE. Secretary? What about Agnes?
MRS BARLOW (*moving down* L) I sacked Agnes that morning. I see she kept mum about that. Irene Morgan arrived about five-thirty. All she had in the world was a tatty little suitcase.
ELIOT. She looks so much like you.
MRS BARLOW (*crossing to Eliot*) Yes, it rather amused me. Later, I thought, "Now Eliot can be unfaithful to two of me."
DENISE. Why didn't anyone miss her?
MRS BARLOW. She's completely alone in the world. I wanted to get away that day, and Irene Morgan was quite willing to go to Paris immediately.
DENISE. When the living-room caught fire, where were you?
MRS BARLOW. Sorry, Denise. I was upstairs packing my things. I'd left the Morgan girl down here, gathering up my papers. (*She moves* C) When I heard the explosion, I ran downstairs and saw the flames and I panicked. I must have picked up her suitcase and I ran from the house and kept on running. (*She sits in the desk chair*) Next morning I read in the paper that Paula Barlow was in hospital. I hesitated a little, but later when I read that she'd lost her memory . . .
DENISE (*moving to* R *of Mrs Barlow*) So you've been sitting in Dover, laughing at us all this time.
MRS BARLOW. No, not all the time. I took a job as Irene Morgan. And I've been writing—and waiting.
ELIOT. What will your public think of you running away and staying away all this time?
MRS BARLOW (*blandly*) I'll explain everything when the Press arrive. Think of the splash the headlines will make tomorrow. "Novelist Traps Husband and Murderous Mistress."
DENISE. You can't prove a thing—no-one can!
MRS BARLOW. Between Irene Morgan and myself, we can easily prove attempted murder. You go to gaol a long time for that.

DENISE (*moving* C) I'm not going to gaol. Eliot—tell her! I won't—will I?

MRS BARLOW. Don't expect my husband to help you. Why do you think he's put up with you this long? Only because he doesn't dare let you out of his sight.

ELIOT (*sharply*) Don't listen to her, Denise.

MRS BARLOW (*to Denise*) You're next on the list, you know. He won't be safe until you've had a fatal accident.

DENISE (*facing Eliot in horror*) Eliot . . . ?

(ELIOT *is silent*)

Then it's true? (*Still unanswered, she breaks*) And I loved you. I really loved you.

(DENISE *turns in anguish and exits into the hall*)

MRS BARLOW. There goes the witness for the crown.

(ELIOT *turns towards her menacingly. The front-door bell rings*)

Answer the door, Eliot.

ELIOT (*pausing*) All right. (*He moves towards the hall*)

(GUTHRIE *enters from the hall*)

GUTHRIE (*moving to* R *of the stairs*) What's going on, Eliot? Where's Irene Morgan?

ELIOT. She's in the study.

MRS BARLOW. I don't expect you to be surprised, Jim. But aren't you glad to see me?

GUTHRIE. I'll survive the shock. (*He crosses to the study door*)

MRS BARLOW. That's a splendid welcome for somebody who's returned from limbo.

GUTHRIE (*stopping and turning*) What do you expect, Paula? Cheering crowds and a special on the B.B.C.?

ELIOT (*moving above the divan*) What made you come back, Jim?

GUTHRIE. I found a letter waiting for me at home. When I read it, I headed straight back here.

ELIOT. From Irene Morgan? Accusing Denise?

GUTHRIE. No, Eliot. Accusing you. It was from Paula in Dover telling me everything that's happened.

(GUTHRIE *exits to the study.* ELIOT *crosses to the stairs*)

MRS BARLOW. Where are you going, Eliot?

ELIOT. I'm going to pack my things.

MRS BARLOW. I think you'd better wait.

(TOD *enters from the garden*)

TOD (*moving to Mrs Barlow*) Paula, darling, let me look at you!

(ELIOT *moves to the bar*)

SCENE 2 PORTRAIT OF MURDER

I thought my heart would burst when I heard your voice on the line. It leaped into my throat like a trout.

MRS BARLOW. Don't get maudlin', Tod. It's hardly your forte.

TOD. You look wonderful, my pet, marvellous. But so like you to risk giving me a coronary.

MRS BARLOW (*crossing below the divan*) Nonsense, Tod, we're both indestructible.

(TOD *stays above the desk chair*.
GUTHRIE *enters from the study*)

GUTHRIE. Eliot, are you responsible for what happened to her?

MRS BARLOW. How is she?

GUTHRIE. Badly shaken, but not seriously, I hope, for all your sakes.

MRS BARLOW. Don't blame me. They tried to kill me. I'm lucky to be alive.

GUTHRIE. You always were lucky, Paula. I'm taking her away from here now. (*He turns to go*)

MRS BARLOW. Jim, before you go—I've finished the novel. Quite the best thing I've ever done.

GUTHRIE. Busy, weren't you?

MRS BARLOW. And I'm half-way through the story of Irene Morgan alias Paula Barlow. We'll go over everything tomorrow.

GUTHRIE. Get yourself another agent, Paula. I represent writers —not boa-constrictors.

(GUTHRIE *exits to the study*)

MRS BARLOW (*crossing to* L) Did you carry out my instructions, Tod?

TOD. The reporters and photographers are already on their way from London, angel.

MRS BARLOW (*sitting in the desk chair*) And the police?

TOD (*moving* C) I've informed the Chief Constable's office. The police will be here. Now, tell me every little detail. Where you've been. What you've done. Each exciting moment.

MRS BARLOW (*rising*) All in good time, Tod. (*She moves to the stairs*) I have to change.

TOD. But, *carita*, the Press and the police will be here at any minute.

MRS BARLOW. I can't meet them as Irene Morgan. Entertain my husband. He could do with cheering up.

(MRS BARLOW *exits up the stairs*)

TOD (*crossing to sit in the desk chair*) You know, Eliot, I can't decide which calamity I prefer for you. Seeing you go to gaol, or seeing you go out and look for a job.

ELIOT. Don't start predicting, Logan. Nothing's going to happen to me. Absolutely nothing.

(GUTHRIE *and* IRENE MORGAN *enter from the study*)

GUTHRIE. You'll hear from us, Eliot. Irene has a lot to settle with you and your wife.

(GUTHRIE *and* IRENE *cross and exit into the hall.* ELIOT *moves and sits in the armchair* R)

TOD. Does your girl-friend know about this development, Eliot? Denise will soon wither away in prison denim, you know. So will you, for that matter.

ELIOT (*calmly*) Logan, you're an interfering old gossip. I've always thought if I ever leaned against you my arm would sink into sour custard up to the elbow.

TOD. Never could stomach me, could you? Just what will you say to the police? Something light and debonair—or a *Mea Culpa* confession out of Dostoievsky?

ELIOT. The Crown needs more than circumstantial evidence to prove a case of attempted murder.

TOD. You can't wave away your hanky-panky with Denise. I'll gladly testify to your goings-on.

ELIOT. Logan, if hanky-panky were a criminal offence, half the population of England would be behind bars.

TOD (*moving and leaning over the back of the divan*) You actually believe you'll get away with it? Eliot, you're hallucinating.

(MRS BARLOW *enters on the stairs. Having undressed, she holds a négligée in front of her to shield her nudity*)

MRS BARLOW. Oh, Tod darling!

TOD (*moving to the stairs*) Yes, angel?

MRS BARLOW. If the Press or the police arrive before I come down, ask them to be patient.

TOD. Do hurry, Paula. It's no time to be preening. And I'm dying to hear your saga.

MRS BARLOW. Get Eliot to tell you. He can start practising for his appearance at the Old Bailey.

(MRS BARLOW *exits at the top of the stairs*)

TOD (*turning to Eliot*) What was your motive? Unbridled passion —or simply cold, hard cash?

ELIOT. There'll be no question of motive. After the way Paula's used Irene Morgan, she doesn't dare go into court.

TOD (*sitting in the desk chair*) You're awfully smug for a man who came close to hanging.

ELIOT. Not very close. The Crown need a *corpus delicti* for that.

(*TV music is heard from the bathroom upstairs, not too loud at first, and unobtrusive*)

TOD. You're deluding yourself, Eliot. (*He rises and moves below the divan*) The Press and police will be here any minute. They won't swallow your lies.

(*The music becomes louder, strident and dissonant*)

(*He reacts peevishly*) What in the name of Bartok is she listening to? (*He moves quickly to the stairs and calls*) Paula! For heaven's sake, angel.
MRS BARLOW (*off upstairs; calling*) What is it, Tod?
TOD. Change that caterwauling. Get something else, can't you?
ELIOT (*rising and moving slowly up* C; *sharply*) Logan, shut up!
MRS BARLOW (*off*) TV in the bathroom—I find it fascinating.
TOD. Well, stir your lovely body and change it before you drive me screaming into the night.
ELIOT. You bloody, meddling fool! (*He lunges for the stairs*)

(TOD *backs to the bar*)

(*He calls and starts frantically up the stairs*) Paula! *Paula!* Don't move—stay where you are! Don't touch it!

(ELIOT *is half-way up the stairs when the music stops abruptly.* MRS BARLOW, *off, screams agonizingly. The* LIGHTS *go out, except for the light on the area around the garden door.* ELIOT *stands frozen on the stairs. There is a shocked silence*)

TOD (*moving to the stairs*) Eliot—Eliot, what's wrong? (*Shrill with panic*) What's happened, Eliot?
ELIOT. She's dead.

CURTAIN

FURNITURE AND PROPERTY LIST

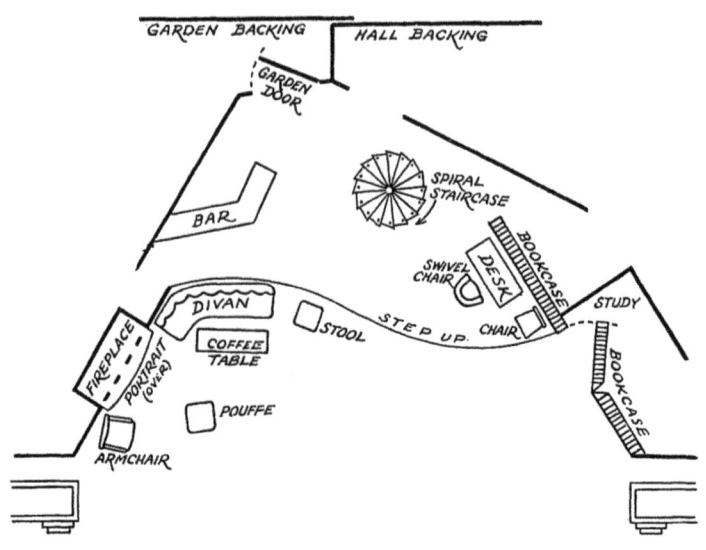

ACT I

Scene 1

On stage: Armchair (down R)
Section of divan (RC)
Low coffee-table. *On it:* table-lighter, ashtray
Sectioned divan. *On it:* cushions
Fire grate with logs
Portrait of Paula Barlow
Bar. *On it:* table-lamp, white telephone, bowl of flowers, 4 glasses, bottle of gin, decanter of whisky, soda syphon, ashtray
On wall behind her: candle-lamp wall-bracket
Stool (C)
High-backed swivel armchair
Upright chair
Writing-desk. *On it:* table-lamp, book, 3 letters for signing, pen in holder, ashtray, other suitable dressing

Door L ajar
Other doors closed
Light fittings off

Off stage: Bunch of white carnations (TOD)
Pile of unopened letters (TOD)
2 suitcases (ELIOT)
Vase with white carnations (AGNES)
Small suitcase (ELIOT)
Portable typewriter (AGNES)

Personal: AGNES: horn-rimmed glasses, typescript
ELIOT: box with diamond-set wedding ring, cigar, matches

SCENE 2

Strike: Flowers and vase of carnations from bar

Set: On bar: fresh flowers
Door L ajar
Other doors closed
Light fittings off

Off stage: Letter (AGNES)
Typescript (MRS BARLOW)
Gift-wrapped package. *In it:* filmy nightdress (AGNES)

Personal: ELIOT: watch, wallet with bank-note
AGNES: newspaper clipping
MRS BARLOW: lighted cigarette

SCENE 3

Strike: Nightdress and packing
Dirty glasses

Set: On coffee-table: large carton. *In it:* TV set, card
Clean glasses on bar
On desk: typed letters
Garden door open
Door L ajar
Light fittings off

Off stage: Letters for post (AGNES)

Personal: AGNES: shoulder bag

ACT II

Scene 1

Strike: Letters from bar
Doors closed
Light fittings on

Off stage: Contracts (GUTHRIE)
Overnight bag (AGNES)
Bouquet of red roses (TOD)
Vase of red roses (TOD)

Personal: GUTHRIE: watch
TOD: 2 letters
During 1st BLACK-OUT
Change flowers on bar

Set: newspaper on coffee-table

During 2nd BLACK-OUT
Change flowers on bar

Strike: Newspaper
During 3rd BLACK-OUT
Change flowers on bar

Strike: Vase of roses from desk
During 4th BLACK-OUT
Change flowers on bar

Reset: Vases of roses on desk

Scene 2

Study door open
Other doors closed
Light fittings on

Off stage: Sheaf of letters (ELIOT)
Suitcase (MRS BARLOW)

Personal: DENISE: letter

LIGHTING PLOT

Property fittings required: wall-bracket, 2 table-lamps, log fire
Interior. A living-room. The same scene throughout
THE MAIN ACTING AREAS are R, RC, LC and up C
THE APPARENT SOURCES OF LIGHT are general daylight and at night, table-lamps R and L and a wall-bracket up RC

ACT I, SCENE 1. An August morning

To open: The stage in darkness

Cue 1	After rise of CURTAIN *Bring in spotlight to pin-point portrait* R	(Page 1)
Cue 2	Follows above cue *Bring in general lighting for daylight effect*	(Page 1)
Cue 3	ELIOT: ". . . without any mistake." *Snap* BLACK-OUT	(Page 11)

ACT I, SCENE 2. Afternoon

To open: Effect of sunshine
Fittings off

Cue 4	PAULA: ". . . old life ended." *Commence slow dim of all lights*	(Page 15)
Cue 5	PAULA: ". . . six every morning." BLACK-OUT	(Page 15)
Cue 6	AGNES: ". . . in the living-room." *Bring up all lights as at opening*	(Page 16)
Cue 7	AGNES: ". . . head in it." *Commence dim of all lights*	(Page 18)
Cue 8	MRS BARLOW: ". . . references from me." BLACK-OUT	(Page 18)
Cue 9	Follows above cue *Bring up all lights as at opening*	(Page 18)
Cue 10	ELIOT: "You are." *Snap* BLACK-OUT	(Page 24)

ACT I, SCENE 3. Late afternoon

To open: Effect of sunshine
             Fittings off

Cue 11   PAULA: "... help me, help me."   (Page 30)
            Snap BLACK-OUT

ACT II, SCENE 1. Evening

To open: Effect of artificial light
             Dark outside garden door
             Light fittings on

Cue 12   GUTHRIE: "... I don't want to."   (Page 34)
            Commence dim of all lights

Cue 13   GUTHRIE: "... them about it."   (Page 34)
            BLACK-OUT

Cue 14   GUTHRIE: "... shortly before noon."   (Page 35)
            Bring up all lights as at opening

Cue 15   MRS BARLOW: "... we're finished!"   (Page 38)
            Commence dim of all lights

Cue 16   MRS BARLOW sits on divan   (Page 38)
            BLACK-OUT

Cue 17   Follows above cue   (Page 38)
            Bring up lights as at opening

Cue 18   PAULA: "Wasn't it?"   (Page 41)
            Commence dim of all lights

Cue 19   TOD: "... that afternoon."   (Page 41)
            BLACK-OUT

Cue 20   TOD: "... garden, as usual."   (Page 41)
            Bring up lights as at opening

Cue 21   MRS BARLOW: "... sorry for me, Tod."   (Page 45)
            Commence dim of lights

Cue 22   MRS BARLOW: "... at her somehow."   (Page 45)
            BLACK-OUT

Cue 23   Follows above cue   (Page 45)
            Bring up lights as at opening

Cue 24   At end of Scene   (Page 47)
            BLACK-OUT

ACT II, SCENE 2. Night

To open: Effect of artificial light

Table-lamp R, on
Table-lamp L, off
Wall-bracket off

Cue 25   Lamp R is knocked over   (Page 50)
          Snap out lamp R
          Take out lights except for the spotlight on the portrait and
              light around the garden door up C

Cue 26   ELIOT switches on wall-brackets and desk lamp   (Page 52)
          Snap in wall-bracket and desk lamp
          Snap in covering lights

Cue 27   MRS BARLOW screams   (Page 57)
          BLACK-OUT *all lights except for the spotlight on the portrait*
              and the area around the garden door

EFFECTS PLOT

ACT I

Scene 1

Cue 1	At rise of CURTAIN *Eerie musical theme sneaks in softly*	(Page 1)
Cue 2	As general lighting comes up *Music builds*	(Page 1)
Cue 3	Follows above cue *Fade music* *Bring in sound of typewriter* L	(Page 1)
Cue 4	TOD: ". . . wherever you are!" *Stop typewriter*	(Page 1)
Cue 5	ELIOT: ". . . I promise." *Front-door bell rings off* R	(Page 7)
Cue 6	PAULA: "Thank you, Eliot." *Telephone rings*	(Page 9)

Scene 2

Cue 7	GUTHRIE: ". . . up in smoke." *Sound of typewriter*	(Page 12)
Cue 8	ELIOT: ". . . you don't mind." *Sound of typewriter ceases*	(Page 12)
Cue 9	PAULA: ". . . like everyone else." *Soft music*	(Page 15)
Cue 10	ELIOT: ". . . when we meet." *Fade music*	(Page 16)
Cue 11	AGNES: ". . . me any consideration?" *Soft music*	(Page 18)
Cue 12	MRS BARLOW: ". . . references from me." *Music comes up strongly*	(Page 18)
Cue 13	The lights come up *Fade music*	(Page 18)

Cue 14	AGNES: ". . . your bedroom extension." *Front-door bell rings*	(Page 19)

SCENE 3

Cue 15	ELIOT: "No risk at all." *Telephone rings*	(Page 28)

ACT II

SCENE 1

Cue 16	GUTHRIE: ". . . I don't want to." *Soft music*	(Page 34)
Cue 17	GUTHRIE: ". . . . shortly before noon." *Fade music*	(Page 35)
Cue 18	MRS BARLOW: ". . . over every word." *Soft music*	(Page 38)
Cue 19	The LIGHTS come up *Fade music*	(Page 41)
Cue 20	TOD: ". . . never on you." *Soft music*	(Page 41)
Cue 21	MRS BARLOW enters *Fade music*	(Page 41)
Cue 22	TOD: ". . . natural assumption is . . ." *Front-door bell rings*	(Page 42)
Cue 23	MRS BARLOW: "Oh—it's you." *Telephone rings*	(Page 43)
Cue 24	TOD: ". . . what she wants." *Soft music*	(Page 45)
Cue 25	The LIGHTS come up *Fade music*	(Page 45)
Cue 26	TOD exits *Telephone rings*	(Page 46)

Scene 2

Cue 27	**Denise** exits *Front-door bell rings*	(Page 54)
Cue 28	**Eliot**: ". . . for that." *TV music (off upstairs)*	(Page 56)
Cue 29	**Tod**: ". . . swallow your lies." *The music becomes louder, strident and dissonant*	(Page 57)
Cue 30	**Eliot** goes up the stairs *Music stops abruptly*	(Page 57)

www.ingramcontent.com/pod-product-compliance
Ingram Content Group UK Ltd.
Pitfield, Milton Keynes, MK11 3LW, UK
UKHW021846210426
5322IPUK00022B/503